마음의 꽃수들

시로 풀어보는 천수경 · 금강경

FLOWER FANCY WORKS OF MIND

마음의 꽃수들

시로 풀어보는 천수경 · 금강경

FLOWER FANCY WORKS OF MIND

Poem : Kim, Youn-Ock (김윤옥)

Art Work : Kim, Youn-Ock (김윤옥)

교육과학사

서문

이 시를 읽고 무슨 의미인지 몰라도 좋아요.
옳다, 그르다 따지지 말고
여러분 자신에게 “이게 무엇이지?”라고 물어보세요.
책 읽는 가운데 어느 한 구절이라도 “아! 이거지!” 하는 순간이 생기면
그것만으로 족합니다.

제1부의 주제인 천수경은 관세음보살의 자비를 닮고자 한국불교에서 만든 경입니다.
그중 요체는 신묘장구 대다라니입니다.
신묘장구 대다라니는 관세음보살의 자비 실천을 담은 것이니
시간 나시는 대로 읽고 외워보세요.
수천 년 전의 발자취이니
글자의 의미를 따르지 말고 관세음보살의 선을 한 번에 깨치기 바랍니다.
부디 관세음보살처럼 자비를 베푸소서.

제2부의 주제는 금강경이며, 금강경은 깨지지 않는 다이아몬드 같은 부처님 설법이니
오직 정각(anyokdarasammaksambori)을 얻기 위함입니다.
이 경을 읽고 이해하거나 이 경 속에 나오는 사구게를 이해하여 남에게 설명한다면
재물로 보시하는 복덕보다 더 큰 복덕을 받는다고 합니다.
읽어 보시고 마음에 와닿는 것이 있으면, 주위 분들과 공유하시기 바라겠습니다.

감사합니다.

2022년 12월
김윤옥

Preface

It is no problem whether you do not understand the meaning of these poems.

Please do not judge whether it is right or wrong.

Just ask yourself "What is this?"

If "Ah! This is it!" moment arises while reading these poems,

The author would be satisfy happily.

The Cheonsugyoung (the Part I theme) is the Sutra which Korean Buddists made in order to practice the mercy of the Gwanseum Bosal (the Goddess of Mercy).

Among the Sutra, the key point is the Magic and Mysterious Great Darani (Sinmyojanggu Daedarany).

It describes the practices of the Goddess of Mercy,

Just recite it whenever you got a time.

It includes the foot traces of the Bosal thousands of years ago,

Please do not mind each meaning literally, and get to enlighten the good at once.

Please practice mercy around like the Goddess of Mercy.

The Part Two theme is from the Unbreakable Diamond Sutra (Geumkangkyoung), which contains the Buddha teaching and speeches.

The Sutra leads readers to understand the highest and right enlightenment (anyokdarasammaksambori).

If you read and understand this Sutra and / or the key points of the Sutra and explain them to others, your reward of virtue is outstanding than whom donated treasures to others.

If you read these poems and some are impressive to you, please share them others around you.

Thank you.

December 2022.

Kim, Youn-Ock

차례

Part I :

도심의 꽃수들
City Flower Fancy Works of Mind

세존 설법

어떤 논리로도 이의를 달 수 없는
극단적인 예로써 물으신다
'아주 그러하다'의 답에 펼쳐지는 말씀

경이나 조로도 헤아릴 수 없는
엄청난 부를 머뭄 없이 보시하라신다
그러나 부처님 경전을 전함이 더 복이 크다는 말씀

'이것이 법이다'라고 말할 수 없는
수많은 경우의 수로 물으신다
세월에 무색하지 않도록 담금질하는 말씀

수많은 각도에서의 질문으로 오해의 소지가 없는
오래 살아남는 원리를 물으신다
몇 천 년이 흘러도 수긍할 수 있는 말씀

Red Camellia

Buddha's 'How-to-Teach'

Any logic could not raise an exception to the Buddha's rules
Buddha casts extreme examples
'Simply agree' invites out–spreading Buddha's words

Could not count beyond billions or trillions of riches
He asks you to devote that much to others
But to impart his words to others is more blessed lives

Could not say "This is the Act" according to Buddha's words
Buddha asks you with numbers of cases
His words immerse deeply not to perish true meaning over times

In order not to misunderstand, questioning in many angles
He asks principles which would survive over thousands of years
Could agree with his Words over thousands of years

불멸의 교훈

내가 어떻게 했는데 이래
'나'라는 생각에
생기는 emotional response

사람이 어떻게 그래
'사람'이라는 생각에
생기는 emotional response

세상이 어떻게 이래
'중생'이라는 생각에
생기는 emotional response

산다는 게 뭐 이래
'존재'라는 생각에
생기는 emotional response

Dandelion

기원전 6세기경 출현 이래
제4차 산업혁명을 영위하는 현재
생각에도
항상 반성하며 살라는 각자의
emotional response

Imperishable Lessons

How have I done to you, why you do that to me
With thinking of 'Me'
Forms 'Me' emotional response

How a person does things like that to a human
With thinking of 'Person(Human)'
Forms 'Person(Human)' emotional response

How people do things like that to humankind
With thinking of 'Humankind'
Forms 'Humankind' emotional response

Pray for longer lifespan
With thinking of 'Lifespan'
Forms 'Lifespan' emotional response

From Buddha came in the world
To present mind that lives in the industry 4.0 world
Live your life with reflections on those emotional response

세상을 겪으니까

사랑이 변한다
한때 뜨겁던 마음에 세상을 겪으니
서로를 재어 본다

우애도 변한다
서로의 마음에 상을 만들고 겪으니
얼마만큼이었는지 재어 본다

우정도 변한다
서로 다른 삶의 무게에 세상을 겪으니
얼마만큼 통하는지 재어 본다

신뢰가 변한다
너와 나의 삶에 세상을 겪으니
나는 너에게 얼마만큼이었는지 재어 본다

Rhododendron Indicum

Because of Living Experience

Love is discolored
Through dating experiences with passion
Begins calculation on each transaction

Sibling–hood also is discolored
Through making images on each other's affection
Begins calculation on each transaction

Friendship is discolored
Through different weigh of living tension
Begins calculating how understand each other's communication

Trust is discolored
Through experiencing one's own life occasion
Calculates how much worth am I to your mind immersion

피안

철쭉을 분해하면 꽃잎 한 조각, 잎, 가지만 있을 뿐 철쭉은 없고
일체 만물은 단지 인연생기(因緣生起)일 뿐
색즉시공 공즉시색
모든 법은 시작도 끝도 없는 것

마을 철쭉 다발 모양을 보고 사진을 찍고
바위틈에서 꽃다발처럼 잘 가꾸었을 뿐
꽃 지면 눈길 주지 않을 마음
마음도 인연생기일 뿐! 인과의 고리에 의한 것

예쁜 철쭉 색깔과 꽃다발 같은 모양을 보지 말고
지성을 비우고 직관하는 지혜는 반야
편견과 선입견은 비우고
눈 / 코 / 귀 / 입 등의 지각양식을 극복하는 지혜인 것

Azalea

일체의 분별을 떠날 수 있는 지혜를 닦고
지혜가 피안에 도달하고
삶과 죽음의 경계에서 일체의 분별망념을 멸하고
이것을 아는 것이 반야바라밀다의 세계인 것

State of Enlightenment

Flower leave, leaves, and stems are azalea's components
There is no azalea if it's divided into a piece of each component
So matter including body is void while vanity is void
Vanity is also matter without beginning nor end

To see and take picture of city Azalea bunches on roads
Appreciate a bouquet of azalea beside the pavement
Turn one's eyes when flowers fallen and disappeared
So mind is a ring of cause and effect derived

Not to see pretty color and shape of azalea bunches
Buddha wisdom is to have an intuition without one's perception preoccupied
Vacate prejudices and preconceptions in the mind
Wisdom overcome perception styles through eyes, nose, ears, and mouth

Knowing status without differentiating all kinds
Then wisdom enters the state of enlightenment
Exterminate each delusive mind
Knowing this is the prajna-paramita world

난초

4월 초에 난초가 화단에 피고
뒤뜰에 핀 난초에 인적 드물고
품은 뜻은 청결한 군자의 성품이니
매/난/국/죽 문인화의 대상품이었으니

한 송이 꽃만 피운 난초꽃은 향기롭고
군자들의 서재에 환영받고
무리 지어 꽃 핀 난초는 화단에 덩그러니
무관심과 겨울 뚫고 피었으니

문인들은 난을 치면서 평정심을 기도하고
수리수리 마하수리 수수리 사바하
수리수리 마하수리 수수리 사바하
입으로 짓는 죄를 깨끗이 해 달라고 비니

한량없는 손과 눈을 가지신 관세음보살이시여
넓고 크고 걸림 없는 대자비심으로
일체중생을 이롭게 하고 안락하게 하시니
정등각을 얻게 도우시는 보살님이시여

Orchid

Orchid

Early April let orchid bloom alone in the garden with other flowers
A few cares orchid flowers in backyard garden
Its meaning implies pure mind of scholar or wise men
So it became an object of Korean literary artists back then

Orchid with only one flower smells sweet when it blooms
So welcome by wise men's study rooms from any garden
Orchid with many flowers are left in the garden with ignorance
So be bloomed out of cold winter and ignorance

Literary artists pray for clean mind while drawing orchids
Surisuri mahasuri susuri sabaha
Surisuri mahasuri susuri sabaha
Please clean the guilt by the speeches spoken

To the Buddhist Goddess of Mercy who has limitless hands and eyes
The Gwan-Se-Um Bosal with wide, huge, and no trapping mercies
Please be beneficial and comfortable for all human beings
Please let them get into the states of enlightenment

낮-달맞이꽃

도시 아파트 화단 바위틈에
오롯이 핀 낮–달맞이꽃에
신기하게도 눈에 띄는 꽃이여

몇 송이가 한 줄기에
동서남북 가리키는 네 개의 분홍 꽃잎에
노란 꽃술 가진 꽃이여

어떤 연고로 이 도시–정원에
이주하여 바위틈에
둥지를 틀고 도시인들에게 인사하는 꽃이여

Day Sun-drops

동서남북과 중앙에
팔방과 중앙에
모든 신에게 올리는 참된 진언이여

사방팔방 이십–사방에
심산의 바위에서 도시–정원에
나무 사만다 못다남 옴 도로도로 지미 사바하

Day Sun-Drops

At space between rocks in a city garden
The day-sun-drops flowers bloomed alone
As by magic, the flowers catch my eyes

A few flowers at a stem in the garden
A pink flower looks like pointing east-west-south-north with stamen
Its yellow stamen exposes

What kind of reason you came in this garden
How you moved into between rocks in a city-garden
Then bloom and say hello to urban citizens

East-west-south-north with center taken
To eight directions and center taken
Sincerely pray to all of Buddhas with true words

Everywhere and twenty-four direction taken
From very high mountains to a urban garden
Sing 'Namu samanda mot-danam om dorodoro jimi sabaha' three times

경전을 찬탄하는 노래

길을 걷다가 꽃잔디 만난 인연
삭막한 뒤뜰 나무들 사이에 피었으니
그 존재감이 빛난다

부처님이 깨달은 법을 만난 인연
위 없이 깊고 깊은 미묘한 법은 망상과 집착을 버리면 만나니
완전히 아름다운 세계가 펼쳐진다

너무나 긴 시간 동안 만나기 어려운 인연
이제야 깨달음을 얻을 가능성을 만났으니
아상을 내려놓으면 행복한 순간이 온다

보리심 실천의 시작된 인연
내가 지금 듣고 보고 얻었으니
받아 지니니 행복의 시작이다

Moss-Pink

나와 부처님 말씀의 인연
믿고 이해하며 체득하니
여래의 진실한 뜻을 얻기를 원한다

Song of Admiring the Buddhist Scriptures

Connection to see moss-pink while taking a walk
Blossomed between trees in a desolate backyard
The presence is highlighted

Connection to meet the Buddhist enlightenment talk
Abandoning delusion and obsession let meet the mysterious end
Then the fully beautiful world is approached

Connection to meet the scripture for long long time to seek
Now I meet a possibility to enlighten through Buddhahood
The happy moment comes when giving up the selfishness concentrated

The aspiration for Buddhahood begins to pick
Now I gain the momentum while I read and heard
The happiness has begun by the moment requested

Connection between the Buddha's words and my pick
Believe and take it then learn by practicing the Word
The real meaning of Buddha's Word is wanted

법장을 여는 진언

척박한 바위틈에 핀 산철쭉 몇 송이
무리 지어 피지 않아도 예쁘구나
수줍은 주황-분홍으로 눈길을 사로잡는구나

큰 바위를 감싸 안은 줄기에 몇 송이
바위틈 사이엔 작은 조각 돌과 흙 조금 있구나
건조한 날씨에 잘도 피었구나

5월의 산에서나 피는 산철쭉 꽃송이
어이타 도시 아파트 정원의 바위틈에 피었나
바위들이 올 때 따라 왔나

Mountain-Azalea

산에 가지 않아도 보게 된 산철쭉 꽃송이
여름을 여는 날씨에 피었구나
한량없는 손과 눈을 가지신 관세음보살이 보내셨구나

관세음보살께서 설법을 여는 세 마디 말씀이
'옴 아라남 아라다'이구나
경전을 설하시기 전에 두 번 더 외치시는구나

Proposing to Begin with the Words of Buddha

A few flowers blossomed on barren soil between rocks
Pretty although you do not blossom in bunches
Catching my eyes with shy orange-pink

A few flowers on a stem hugging rocks
There are a few dirt and little pebbles
Well blossomed in dry weather with wink

Mountain-Azalea supposed to be in May among mountain rocks
How come you blossomed in a garden of city Apt. complexes
Did you come along with rocks from a mountain to the garden rank

Connection to see you although we do not climb a mountain rocks
Blossomed here in the season of opening Summer times
The Goddess of Mercy with limitless hands and eyes blow you by blink

Recite three phrases before the Gwan-Se-Um Bosal speaks
'Om aranam arada' that the Bosal recites
Then two more times recited before teaching a sacred book

양지꽃처럼

부처님 오신 달에 도처에 양지꽃이 피었네
음력 4월의 뉴그린 속의 노랑 꽃잎이
조화롭고 평화롭구나

절마다 빨강, 노랑, 주황 연등을 달았네
병 없이 오래 살기를 원하는 소원이
우리 모두에게 제일의 염원이구나

원근, 전후, 상하, 주야 훤히 볼 수 있는 눈으로 보시네
절마다 등에 붙어있는 각각의 소원이
양지꽃처럼 지천으로 널려 있구나

Cinqfoil

넓고 큰 만족을 구하기를 비네
막히거나 그치는 것이 없이
성취하기를 비는구나

부처님 제자 중 대비심이 가장 큰 관세음보살께 비네
대다라니 경에 대한 암송이
관자재보살께 아뢰어 청하는 길이구나

Like Cinqfoil

Cinqfoil blossomed everywhere on the Buddha's birthday month
Yellow flowers among the new-green in lunar April
How are harmonious and peaceful

Temples hang red, yellow, orange lotus lanterns for the Buddha's birth
Praying the wish for long lives without ill
It would be a first wish for us to get in hopeful

Clearly near-far, back-front, top-bottom, and day-night she sees our oath
Each wish hanging to each lotus lantern to be fulfill
They are spread out everywhere like cinqfoil in the grass full

We pray for obtaining a wide, and big satisfaction to have faith
Without blocking and being clogged when trying to fulfill
Pray for achieving the wish as turned out to be successful

Pray to the most mercy Goddess among Buddha's disciples with oath
Reciting the great Darani as a her pupil
We tell and ask the Gwan-Se-Um Bosal for the state of being mindful

노란 창포의 꽃 공양

연못가에 핀 창포가 화려한 노란 머리 하고
중생들에게 계절의 미를 베푸는 꽃 공양
무수히 많은 연잎들도 노래하는 계절에 대한 경배심

관세음보살의 대다라니에 머리 숙여 귀의하고
대다라니는 부처님께 바치는 법공양
대다라니는 관세음보살이 실천한 자비심

타인을 위해 넓고 깊은 원력과 그 모습은 거룩하고
차원 높은 지혜로 중생들의 고통 해결은 양양
타인을 위해 마음 쓰는 원력의 자비심

Jacob's Wort

천 개의 손으로써 우리를 보호하고 감싸주고
중생의 고통과 소원을 들어주는 장엄한 자양
천 개의 손에 주렁주렁 달려있는 자비심

천 개의 눈으로 널리 두루 관찰하여 비추고
중생들에게 자비를 펼치는 데에 의기양양
중생에게 천 개의 눈으로 찾아주는 자비심

Yellow Flowers that Jacob's Wort offer

Jacob's wort with pretty yellow hair blossomed by a pond
Offering season's beautiful flowers to mankind
Hundreds of lotus leave bow in worship to the season

The Goddess of Mercy devoted to the Darani by bending her head
The Great Darani that is devoted to the Buddha to be read
The Great Darani is the very mercy of the Gwan-Se-Um Bosal chosen

Wide-deep enlightening power and holy attitude the Bosal has had
Her higher level of wisdom solve the pains of mankind
The helping power of mercy to take care of others' poison

With thousand hands to protect us and defend
Her great nutrition to relieve pains and wishes of mankind
With her thousand hands hanging mercies in hundreds of dozen

Her thousand eyes highlight and observe over the world
The Bosal is triumphant to give mercy to mankind
She finds mercy-needs with her thousand eyes vision

클로버가 뜻하는 행운과 행복

네 잎 클로버는 행운, 세 잎 클로버는 행복을 뜻하는바
행운을 찾기 위해 무수히 밟아버린 행복은 없었나
클로버 꽃으로 팔찌 만들던 동심은 행복한 본말

관세음보살은 진실한 말 가운데 불가사의한 말씀을 베푸는바
무엇을 베풀어도 베풀었다는 생각이 없는 마음을 닮아 보았나
함(무위)이 없이 저절로 이루어지는 보살님의 정말

중생은 바라는 바를 속히 풀어 달라는바
관세음보살의 자비심이 담긴 대다라니를 암송해봤나
뜻하는 바를 위해 노력하도록 울력이 되는 그 말

지은 죄업은 거미줄처럼 얽혀 자타에게 영향을 주는바
그 인과는 또 다른 과보를 낳아 업장이 두터워짐을 알고 있나
참회를 통해 업장을 소멸시켜 밝음을 찾으라는 당부의 말

인과 법칙은 부처님이 만든 것이 아닌바
진리로 가는 길을 깨달아 그 길을
　가리켜 안내하나
행운을 쫓아 행복을 버리는 중생의 결말

Clover

Luck and Happiness that Clover implies

Clover with four leaves means luck, while three leaves says happiness
Did you happened to step on countless happiness to find luck
Children's innocence making bracelets of clover is happiness itself

The Goddess of Mercy gives mysterious words among truthful words
Have you ever taken after the mercy without expecting to take back
The Bosal does nothing but let you achieve it by yourself

Praying one's wishes quickly to be achieved for which mankind asks
Have you ever recited the Great Darani of the Bosal book
The wishes could be achieved by our steady tries under her boundary roof

We are affected by our committing sins complicated like spiderwebs
Do you know the cause-effect connected to another sin getting thick
Buddha asks to extinct the karma by letting it go and reset yourself

Buddha did not create law of cause and effect stuffs
Only guides us to get there by his enlightenment of the truth to seek
Mankind might end up with getting rid of happiness to find luck stuff

삼매의 상태

관세음보살의 자비심이 철쭉처럼 너무 곱고 훌륭해서
천상의 성인들과 용이 지원하며
이미 우리는 자비를 받고 있으며 파도를 극복하도록 하시네

어떤 일을 하든지 그 일과 하나 되어 마음을 비우고 철저히 해서
백천 가지의 일마다 삼매로 수행하며
자기도 모르는 사이에 온갖 수행의 결실을 거두네

이와 같은 관세음보살의 말씀을 지니면 광명의 깃발이 되어서
마음이 든든해지며
이는 부처님의 정신으로 경전의 말씀이라네

부처님 말씀을 수지한 사람의 마음은 신통의 창고를 만들어서
최선을 다하면 자기도 모르는 사이에 그 일은 이루어지며
대다라니의 변화가 그 사람의 마음 가운데 나타난다네

Royal Azalea

마음의 창고 속에 대다라니의 진리를
가득 채워서
자신이 가지고 있는 빛나는 보물에
대해 믿고 이해하며
그러한 보물을 손에 있는 것처럼 볼 수
있어야 하네

The Blissful State of Self-Forgetfulness

The mercies by the Gwan-Se-Um Bosal are great and beautiful like
royal-azaleas
All saints and magic dragon in the heaven support her
We already get mercy to come over wild sea everywhere

Empty one's mind and constitute a whole with whatever s/he does
Cultivate yourself in blissful state of self-forgetfulness onto each labor
You come to fruition of the cultivation by self-concentration here

Could see the clearest flag by following the Bosal Words
You are getting confident like her
This is the Buddha's spirit which the sacred book inquire

Who goes with the Buddha Words can build marvelous stores
Your hopes can be accomplished as you do best labor
The Mysterious Scripture bring changes in your mind centre

If you save the truth of the Mysterious Scripture in the mind-stores
You believe and understand your own shining treasure power
You should see the treasures as if in your hand store

조팝나무꽃처럼 피는 번뇌

조팝나무는 아무 곳에서나 잘 자라고
그 꽃은 우리의 번뇌처럼 잘 피어서
길가에서도 우리를 반긴다

모든 번뇌를 씻어 버리고
괴로움의 바다를 건너게 해 주소서
관세음보살의 자비를 내 삶으로 하여 온갖 번뇌를 건넙시다

깨달음에 이르는 온갖 방편문을 뛰어넘고
매 순간 조금씩 실천하다 보면 어느 날 놀라운 결과로서
대다라니를 통해서 한 번에 성불의 길로 갑시다

Bridal wreath

지금 관세음보살의 자비를 칭송하고
불교는 자비이며 자비는 관세음보살로 불리니
관세음보살을 칭송하면서 귀의하고자 합니다

우주 법계는 마음의 미세 차이를 다 알아서 결과를
초래하고
내 마음에 따라 결과 오고서
이 깨달음으로 다 이루어지게 하소서

Agonies Blossomed like Bridal Wreath Flowers

Bridal wreath grows well anywhere
The flowers blossom well like our agonies
They would welcome us in any street

Let us wash out each agony from everywhere
Let us cross the sea of pains
Let us jump each agony by taking after the Gwan-Se-Um Bosal

Let us skip all the doors to the very enlightenment figure
What you do little by little every moment brings magic results
Let us become a Buddha at once through the Darani

Here are the Bosal mercies that I admire
Buddhism is to give mercy to others as the Bosal does mercies
By admiring the Bosal I want to devote to be a Buddhist

The laws of space know microscopic differences of mind in sincere
The results appear according to my mind setups
Please let these achieved by this enlightenment

관세음보살께 비는 십향 중 첫 다섯 가지 소원

대자대비하신 관세음보살님께 귀의하오니
나의 본성인 부처로 돌아가는 일체법을 빨리 얻기를 원합니다
원력을 별안간 깨닫기를 원합니다

대자대비하신 관세음보살님께 귀의하오니
지혜의 안목을 빨리 얻기를 원합니다
부처님의 지혜가 저절로 스며들기를 원합니다

대자대비하신 관세음보살님께 귀의하오니
저의 깨달음으로 모든 중생을 제도할 수 있기를 원합니다
부처님처럼 다른 사람들도 다 깨달아지기를 원합니다

Korean Weigela

대자대비하신 관세음보살님께 귀의하오니
다른 사람을 위해 쓸 수 있는 좋은 방법을 빨리
얻기를 원합니다
서로 다른 많은 중생을 제도하는 방법을 원합니다

대자대비하신 관세음보살님께 귀의하오니
분별심을 깨는 지혜의 배에 속히 타기를 원합니다
많은 사람이 함께 얻는 지혜를 원합니다

The First Five Wishes of the Ten to the Goddess of Mercy

I devote to the Goddess of Mercy, Gwan-Se-Um Bosal
Want to exceed all methods to find the original me as Buddha quickly
Want to cultivate at once to awake the state of Buddha

I devote to the Gwan-Se-Um Bosal
Wanting to gain insight of wisdom quickly
Wanting to all parts of me to be permeated with wisdom of Buddha

I devote to the Gwan-Se-Um Bosal
Wanting to be able to save all mankind by my awakening quickly
Wanting other people to be awaken like Buddha

I devote to the Gwan-Se-Um Bosal
Wanting to obtain good methods to use for others quickly
Wanting to use appropriate method to each mankind like Buddha

I devote to the Gwan-Se-Um Bosal
Want to get on the ship of wisdom to break differentiation quickly
Want mankind to gain the wisdom together to get on the Prajna

관세음보살께 비는 십향 중 나머지 다섯 가지

대자대비하신 관세음보살님께 귀의하오니
분별심으로 인한 괴로움의 바다를 속히 건너기를 원합니다
분별심을 깨고 세상의 고통에서 벗어나기를 원합니다

대자대비하신 관세음보살님께 귀의하오니
깨치기 위한 계율, 고요한 마음, 지혜를 얻기를 원합니다
분별심을 내려놓기 위해 삼매를 얻고자 합니다

대자대비하신 관세음보살님께 귀의하오니
빨리 원적산에 오르기를 원합니다
분별심이 완전히 깨진 깨달음의 산에 오르기를 원합니다

Jardins de France

대자대비하신 관세음보살님께 귀의하오니
빨리 집착과 소유욕에서 벗어나기를 원합니다
억지로 하지 않는 본성의 집에서 만나기를 원합니다

대자대비하신 관세음보살님께 귀의하오니
빨리 법의 성품을 가진 몸 즉 부처와 하나가 되기를
원합니다
빨리 성불하기를 원합니다

The Other Five Wishes of the Ten to the Goddess of Mercy

I devote to the Goddess of Mercy, Gwan-Se-Um Bosal
Want to cross the sea of agonies quickly
Want to get out of agonies which caused by differentiating the world

I devote to the Gwan-Se-Um Bosal
Want to earn wisdom, calm, and religious precepts to enlighten quickly
Want to focus on practicing to be calm to put aside differentiating mind

I devote to the Gwan-Se-Um Bosal
Want to enter the place of mindful paradise quickly
Want to climb the Mt. of enlightenment that broke differentiating mind

I devote to the Gwan-Se-Um Bosal
Want to get out of obsession and possessiveness quickly
Want to meet the human nature that does not enforce one's mind

I devote to the Gwan-Se-Um Bosal
Want to have nature of Buddhist writings quickly
Eager to attain Buddhahood

내가 본래의 부처를 깨달으면

내가 만일 뾰족뾰족한 칼로 이루어진 칼산으로 향해 가면
남을 혼내주려거나 해치려는
칼 지옥이 스스로 꺾이고

내가 만일 불같이 뜨거운 물 지옥으로 향해 가면
마음속에 끓는 분노나 화가 나서 미치는
뜨거운 물 지옥이 스스로 말라버리고

내가 만일 지옥으로 향해 가면
집착, 욕심, 어리석음 등으로 괴롭고 힘이 드는
지옥이 스스로 말라서 없어지고

내가 만일 탐욕의 지옥으로 향해 가면
채워도 채워지지 않는
탐욕 지옥은 스스로 만족하게 되고

Love I

내가 만일 사악한 지옥으로 향해 가면
투쟁심, 내 고집으로 언제나 싸우려는
악한 마음이 스스로 굴복하고

내가 만일 짐승의 세계로 향해 가면
본능에만 의존하고 생명의 존귀를 모르는
짐승 같은 마음은 사라지고 스스로
지혜를 얻고

If I awake that I got already Buddhahood

If I go toward mountains covered with sharp knives
To scold, blame, or harm others
Knife mountains are broken themselves

If I go toward boiling water hell like fires
About to crazy by anger or burst into a rage due to others
Angers like boiling water get dry themselves

If I go toward greedy hell like obsessions
Be distressed by obsessive or foolish thoughts
The hell dries up it selves

If I go toward starving ghost hell like demons
Does not satisfy although I fill and fill up my wishes
The greedy hell satisfies it self

If I go toward evil hell like wicked persons
Combative spirit or my stubbornness which is ready to fight always
The evil mind gives in it self

If I go toward animal hell like animal worlds
Dependent on instinct and neglect the worth of lives
The hell mind is disappeared and you can earn wisdom of solutions

관세음보살께 귀의합니다

세상의 모든 소리를 살펴보며
이 세상의 모든 것을 관조하여 보살피고
중생을 이익되게 하는 성자

천 개의 눈과 천 개의 손을 가지며
대자대비의 마음으로 중생을 구제하고
세상을 제도하는 청정한 성자

중생에게 두려움 없는 마음을 베풀며
중생을 연민하는 마음으로 이익되게 하고
내 안에도 이미 존재하는 성자

팔각형의 보타락산에 사신다고 하며
산에서 자라는 꽃과 흐르는 물은 빛과 향기를 내고
사방팔방을 두루 살피기 좋은 정자

관세음보살은 머리에 보관을 쓰고
계시며
한 손에는 버드나무 가지 또는 연꽃을
들고
다른 손에는 정병을 든 성자

Queen Elizabeth

Devote to the Goddess of Mercy

The Goddess of Mercy listens to every sounds in the world
Takes care of everything in the world by observing
Saint giving out benefits to mankind

She has thousand eyes and thousand hands to help mankind
Aids mankind with great mercy giving
Saint takes care of the world

She gives mercy without fear to mankind
Let us take benefits with loving
The Saint lives already in my mind to help out the world

The Mountain is octahedral angles to observe the world
Flowers and spring water are fragrant and shining
The location can see well four and eight directions of the world

She wears crown with treasures on her head
One hand holds willow branch or lotus flower bursting
Saint holds a bottle on the other hand

대세지보살께 귀의합니다

부처님은 자비의 문과 지혜의 문이 있으며
대세지보살은 지혜로 중생을 이끄는 힘을 가지고
관세음보살은 자비로써 부처님을 보좌하는 성자

오른쪽에 있는 대세지보살은 지혜와 광명이 으뜸이며
아미타불의 왼쪽에는 자비하신 관음이 계시고
각각 아미타 삼존불 중의 한 분인 성자

지혜로 중생의 어리석음을 없애주시며
지혜는 메타인지지식과 메타인지기술을 가지며
밝은 지혜로 중생이 지옥 같은 상황을 극복하도록 하는 성자

Charles de Gaule

서방정토 극락세계에서 지혜의 빛으로 널리 중생을 비추시며
무상한 힘으로 중생이 굶주림, 축생, 지옥 등을 극복하게 하시고
발을 디디면 삼천세계의 마군을 항복시키는 성자

정수리에 보병이 있는 천관이 있으며
보병에는 메타인지경험과 모니터링 기술이 가득하고
대세지보살은 중생이 자기규제를 할 수 있도록 무한한 힘을 주시는 성자

Devote to the Daesegy Bosal Who Has Full of Wisdom

Amitabha Buddha has powers of mercy and wisdom
The Daesegy Bosal leads mankind with wisdom powers
The Gwan-Se-Um Bosal gives out endless mercies

The Daesegy Bosal sits on the right from Buddha and the best is wisdom
On the left side the Gwan-Se-Um Bosal having mercy powers
So the Daesegy Bosal is one of the three Buddhas

The Saint gets rid of foolishness of mankind by the wisdom
Which includes full of metacognition knowledge and skills
The bright wisdom aids mankind to overcome hell situations

At the land of happiness the Bosal lights mankind by the wisdom
Let us gain limitless power to overcome starving, animal hell, and evils
The Bosal's stepping surrenders the evils from all the worlds

The Bosal wears a crown with a treasure bottle keeping wisdom
Including full of metacognition experiences and monitoring skills
The Bosal gives limitless power to mankind to self-regulate themselves

관세음보살의 9가지 화신들

천 개의 눈과 천 개의 손으로 중생을 구제하는
나무 천수보살
관음의 6 화신 중 하나

일체 중생의 고통을 구제하고 소원을 성취시키는
사유상을 하고 있는 여의륜보살
육 관음 중의 하나

미혹을 끊는 지혜와 복덕이 매우 큰
번뇌를 깨뜨리고 진리로 이끄는 큰 수레바퀴를 만드는 대륜보살
손에 3고의 금강저를 들고 있는 관음 중의 하나

Princess de Monaco

세상의 소리를 듣고 교화를 돕는 관자재보살
해탈의 길로 빨리 들어서게 하는 정취보살
둥근 달처럼 중생에게 지혜를 찾도록 비추는
만월보살

물에 비친 달처럼 가피력이 어디에서나 비치는
수월보살
감로수 병을 들고 고액을 물리치는 군다리보살
자비, 성냄, 엄포, 미소로 아수라를 구제하는 십일면보살

아홉 화신 외에 모든 큰 보살들을 통칭하는 제대보살
본디 스승이신 본사 아미타불 부처님
아미타불께 귀의합니다

Nine Avatars of the Goddess of Mercy (Gwan-Se-Um Bosal)

Thousand eyes and thousand hands to aide mankind
Are physical characteristic of Cheonsu Bosal Buddhist Saint
Is one of the first six avatars of the Gwan-Se-Um Bosal

Helps achieving wishes and relieves pains of mankind
Thinking image is a unique characteristic of Yeuiryoon Bosal
Is also one of the first six avatars of the Gwan-Se-Um Bosal

Wisdom to cut confusion and the reward of virtue are grand
Breaking agony and authorizing wheel are jobs of Daeryoon Bosal
Is one of the first six avatars of the Gwan-Se-Um Bosal

Edifying Buddhist Saint is Gwanjajae Bosal who listens sounds of the world
Helping in reaching nirvana quickly is Jeongchi Bosal
Wisdom like a full moon is Manwall Bosal as an avatar of the Mercy

Like the moon on the water everywhere the Suwal Bosal helps mankind
Who beats misfortunes by magic water is Goondari Bosal
The Eleven headed Bosal aides mankind with anger, threat, and mercy

And there are other great Bosals called Jaedae Bosal in the Bosal world
The master of Buddhists is Armitabul, Buddha Saint
Let us devote to Armitabul who has powers of wisdom and mercy

신묘장구 대다라니 (I)

보살, 마하살, 대비하신 삼보께, 성 관자재보살께 귀의합니다
일체의 두려움을 구제해 주시는 어진 관음께 귀의하고
예경함으로 성스러운 관자재보살의 위신력이시여

저 청경의 명성이 높은 마음의 주인에 회귀하옵니다
일체의 목적을 성취하고 훌륭함으로 존경하고
일체 귀신들이 이길 수 없는 분이시여

광명론, 광명의 지혜존, 세간을 초월하신 존이시여
위대하신 보살이시여 마음의 진언을 기억하옵고
대승리자시여 수지보존하옵는 대지의 왕 자재존이시여

발동하옵소서. 더러움을 이탈한 존이시여.
무구청정 원만상존이시여 강림하옵고
탐독을 소멸케 하옵는 세계의 주인이시여

진독을 소멸케 하옵소서
어리석음의 독을 소멸케 하옵고
그 독을 어서 빨리 가져가십시오,
존이시여

Twist

The Magic and Mysterious Great Darani (Ⅰ)

Devote to three Budhist saints as saint, Great saint, and Great mercy saint
Devote to benevolent Goddess of Mercy who cures all kinds of fears
Please appear your great power of holy Gwanjajae Saint with respect

Devote to the lord of mind who got fame with blue neck by fight
By outstanding to achieve all purposes
The great saint who can beat all kinds of ghost

Ah! to the Fairness saint, Wisdom saint, Transcend saint
And the Great saint please remember our true mindful words
To the great winner and the lord of earth please preserve almighty gift

Please activate the gift of getting rid of dirty mind-product
Innocent, fresh, and perfect integrity saint, please descends
Lord of the world, please extinct the greedy poison rising from heart

Please extinct the very poison of heart
Please extinct the poison of foolishness
Please take all of these fast

신묘장구 대다라니 (Ⅱ)

관세음이시여 어여삐 여기시어 애욕을 파하도록 힘을 주소서
성취하신 분이시여 성취하게 하소서
위대하게 성취하신 분이시여 성취하게 하소서

요가를 성취하신 자재론이시여, 성취하게 하소서
청정관음이시여 성취하게 하소서
산돼지 얼굴, 사자 얼굴 하신 관음이시여 성취하게 하소서

연꽃을 손에 잡은 관음이시여 성취하소서
큰 수레바퀴를 구족하신 관음이시여 성취하소서
법소리, 나팔소리로 깨닫게 하는 관음이시여 성취하소서

Tancho

큰 곤봉을 가진 관음이시여 성취하소서
왼쪽 어깨에 검은 서상을 하신 관음이시여 성취하소서
호랑이가죽 옷을 입은 관음이시여 성취하소서

삼보님께 귀의하며 성스러운 관음께 귀의하소서
신묘장구 대다라니는 천수경의 핵심이니 암송하소서
관음의 행적, 다양한 모습 등이 담겨있으니 암송하소서

The Magic and Mysterious Great Darani (II)

The Goddess of Mercy, please help us to avoid greedy love
The Winner of achieving, please let us achieve good deeds
The Great St. of achieving, please let us achieve mercy

The Gwanjajae Bosal achieving yoga, please let us have what you achieve
The clean and calm Goddess of Mercy, please let us achieve clean minds
The Goddess of Mercy with pig or lion faced, please let us achieve mercy

The Goddess of Mercy with holding lotus, please let us achieve mercy love
The Goddess with big wheel, please let us achieve good authorizing-wheels
The Bosal letting us realize by bugle note, please let us achieve mercy

The Goddess of Mercy with big cudgel, please let us get what you achieve
The Bosal in black robe on left shoulder, please let forgive our sins
The Bosal wearing tiger skin clothes, please let us win with mercy

Devote to the three Buddhist treasures and holy mercy as the above
The core of the Cheonsu scriptures is the above mercy practices
Includes the Bosal's whereabouts and helping figures to practice mercy

신묘장구 대다라니

나모라 다나다라 야야나막알야 바로기제 새바라야
모지사다바야 마하사다바야 마하가로 니가야
옴 살바 바예수 다라나 가라야
다사명 나막 까리다바 이맘알야 바로기제 새바라
다바 니라간타 나막하리나야
마발다 이사미 살발타 사다남
수반아예염 살바보다남 바바말야 미수다감 다냐타
옴 아로게 아로가 마지로가 지가란제
혜혜하례 마하모지 사다바 사마라 사마라 하리나야
구로구로 갈마 사다야 사다야
도로도로 미연제 마하미연제 다라다라 다린나례 새바라
자라자라 마라 미마라 아마라 몰제예혜혜 로게 새바라
라아 미사미 나사야 나베사 미사미 나사야
모하자라 미사미 나사야
호로호로 마라호로 하례 바나마 나바
사라사라 시리시리 소로소로 못쟈못쟈
모다야모다야 매다라야 니라간타 가마사 날사남 바라
하라나야 마낙 사바하
싯다야 사바하
마하싯다야 사바하
싯다유예 새바라야 사바하
니라간타야 사바하
바라하 목카상하 목카야 사바하
바나마 하따야 사바하

자가라 욕다야 사바하
상카섭나네 모다나야 사바하
마하라 구타다라야 사바하
바마사 간타 이사시체다 가릿나 이나야 사바하
먀가라 잘마이바 사나야 사바하
나모라 다나다라 야야나막알야 바로기제 새바라야사바하
나모라 다나다라 야야나막알야 바로기제 새바라야사바하
나모라 다나다라 야야나막알야 바로기제 새바라야사바하

Summer Lady

The Magic and Mysterious Great Darani (Korean version in English)[1)]

Namora danadara yaya namakalya barogije saebaraya

Mojisadabaya maha sadabaya mahagaro nigaya

Om salba bayesu darana garaya

Dasamyoung namak ggaridaba imamalya barogije saebara daba

Niraganta namak harinaya mabalda isami salbalta sadanam

Subanahyeyoum salbabodanam babamalya misudagam

Danyata Om aroge aroga majiroga jigaranje

Hehehare mahamoji sadaba samara samara harinaya

Guroguro galma sadaya sadaya dorodoro miyounje

Maha-miyounje daradara darinnare saebara

Jarajara mara mimara amara molje-ehehe

Roge saebara Raah misami nasaya

Nabesa misami nasaya

Mohajara misami nasaya Horohoro

Marahoro hare banama naba sarasara sirisiri sorosoro motjamotja modaya modaya

Maedaraya niraganta gamasa nalsanam bara Haranaya manak sabaha

Sitdaya sabaha

Maha sitdaya sabaha

Sitdayuye saebaraya sabaha

---

1) First Letter mnemonics : N MODe NSD H. GM JR. Nabesa M & M
MS MS NiBBan Jag SaM Baby M & 3N

Niragantaya sabaha

Baraha mokkasanha mokkaya sabaha

Banama hattaya sabaha

Jagara yodaya sabaha

Sankaseobnane modanaya sabaha

Mahara gutadaraya sabaha

Bamasa ganta isasicheda garitna inaya sabaha

Myagara jalma-iba sanaya sabaha

Namora danadara yaya namakalya barogije saebaraya sabaha (3 times)

사방찬과 도량찬

관음의 위력이 우주에 충만하기를 바라는 사방찬을 외우고
동남서북 네 방향을 청정하게 하며
도량찬으로 내 자신의 불법(천수경)을 찬탄하고 발원하고
마음의 밭을 수행하기 위해 천수경을 독송하다

동방에 물 뿌리니 불법을 독송하는 내 마음 공간 깨끗하고
남방에 물을 뿌리니 쾌정함이 이루어졌으며
서방에 물을 뿌리니 극락세계 완연하고
북방에 물을 뿌리니 영원히 즐거운 세계로다

Louis de Funes

내 마음 공간 청정하니 관음 위력으로 더러움이 없어지고
천상의 불법을 옹호하는 신이 강림하여 보호하시며
지금 사유 너머의 신묘장구 대다라니를 끝까지 외우고
가호(bless)와 자비를 베풀어 주시길 바라다

Glorifying Four Directions and the Ground of Mind

To fulfill powers of the Mercy, recite the Four Direction Glorification
Clean and Glorify the directions of east, south, west, and north
Pray for my Buddhist words by glorifying the Ground of Mind
Recite the Cheonsu Scripture to practice mind's ground clean

My mind space reciting Buddha scripture is clean by watering east direction
My mind space is getting clear by watering south
By watering west, the Land of Happiness is obvious in deed
It is a forever joyful world by watering north clean

With powers of the Gwan-Se-Um Bosal my mind space gets clarification
The three Buddhist treasures and heaven-dragon come to protect earth
Now I recite the Mysterious Great Darani beyond thinking to the end
The Gwan-Se-Um Bosal's bless and mercy are what I hope to glean

알골드 장미와 참회

알골드 장미는 꽃잎도 많네
이 꽃잎들은 마음대로 구겨져 있고
우리가 봐 왔던 장미 꽃잎들과 달라 보이고

우리는 모두 사회화되어 사네
보호자의 훈육과 국가로부터 교육을 받고
이 사회에서 옳은 것이 저 사회에서는 그른 것도 보고

각자의 삶을 돌아다 보면 후회하는 일이 있네
초등학생일 때는 반성문도 많이 써 보고
어른이 되어선 합리화도 열심히 해 보고

All Gold

과거에 지은 모든 악업은 탐진치(탐욕, 분노, 무지)로
생겨났네
자기가 바라는 것을 탐하고 구하고
자기 감정과 어긋나는 대상에 대해 화내고

어리석음으로 사물의 도리를 모르네
몸, 입, 생각으로 지은 모든 악업은 불행을 일으키는
단초이고
나는 지금 모든 악업을 참회하고 또 참회하고

All-Gold Roses and Confession

All-gold rose has lots of flower leaves
These leaves look like crumpled as one likes
They look like different from other kinds of roses

We live by socialization as our family members
There are parenting and educating from social institutions
Right in this society but might wrong in other sometimes

One might regret when looking back sometimes
One might write confession diary often during elementary years
Adults might usually rationalize one's misbehaviors

All past misdeeds are caused by greedy, angry, and foolish minds
One might chase and be greedy on what s / he wants
One might get angry for others with disagreements

We can not reason things out due to foolishness
All misdeeds by physical, verbal, and thinking deed call misfortunes
Now I beg forgiveness on my guilt and do confessions

골든 하트 장미와 참제업장 12 존불

골든 하트 장미는 일반 정원에 흔하지 않고
우리들의 참회도 흔하지 않고
골드 심장으로 참회 받아주는 12 존불께 읍소하네

나무참제업장보승장불을 부르면 남에게 진 신세와 허물이 소멸하고
보광왕하염조불을 부르면 돈으로 사치하고 낭비한 죄를 용서받고
일체향화자재력왕불을 부르면 한평생 잘못한 모든 죄업이 소멸하네

Golden Heart

백억항하사결정불 부르면 살생한 죄업이 소멸하고
진위덕불 부르면 사음한 죄, 악담한 죄가 소멸하고
금강견강소복괴산불을 부르면 지옥에 떨어질 죄업이 소멸하네

보광월전묘음존왕불을 부르면 설법을 많이 들은 자를 변호하시고
환희장마니보적불을 부르면 평생 성낸 죄업을 소멸하시고
무진향승왕불을 부르면 한량없는 생사의 고통을 소멸하시네

사자월불을 부르면 축생으로 태어날 죄업을 소멸하시고
환희장엄주왕불을 부르면 살생, 도둑질 등 큰 죄업을 소멸하시고
제보당마니보적불을 부르면 탐욕으로 지은 온갖 죄업을 소멸하시네

Golden-Heart Rose and Confession to the 12 Buddhist Saints

Golden-Heart roses are rare to see in general gardens
Likely we might rarely confess
With my golden heart I beg forgiveness to 12 Buddhist saints

The Chamje-eopjangboseongjangbul erases my debts for others' kindness
The Boseonghayeomjobul erases my guilt wasting money and goods
The Ilchehyangwhajajaeryoukwongbul erases all my misbehaviors

The Baekeokhyanghasagyouljeongbul erases my guilt killing animals
The Jinwedeokbul erases my guilt of having affair or curses
The Geumganggyeongangsobokgoisanbul erases my guilt that ought to pay for hell's calls

The Bogwongwaljeonmyoeomjonwongbul pleads me for listening to many lectures on Buddha Words
The Whanheejangmanibojeokbul erases my guilt built by angers
The Mujinhyangseongwangbul erases my pains on live or death

The Sajawalbul erases my karma to be born as an animal beings
The Whanheejangeomjuwongbul erases my guilt by stealing deeds
The Jebodangmanibojeokbul erases my guilt raised by greediness

생명 경시에 대한 참회

노란 장미 꽃말 중에는 완벽한 성취가 있으며
인류는 편리함의 완벽한 성취를 위해 진화하고
그 과정에서 떠내려온 고래의 배에선 플라스틱 쓰레기가 가득

병충해를 막기 위해 농작물에 농약을 뿌리며
사냥철에는 총으로 산 짐승들을 잡고
가끔 개나 사람도 총상으로 죽어서 불가한 납득

도시 고층 아파트 베란다 창틀 위에 말벌이 집을 지으며
창문 열면 들어올까 봐 에프킬라 듬뿍 뿌리고
돌아온 말벌들은 집을 포기하고 나의 목적은 간단히 취득

이 모든 살생은 생명을 경시하는 죄업이며
환경을 해쳐서 결국 인간에게 돌아오고
사회적 갈등과 지구 온난화로 인한 재해를 습득

천년이 지나도 노란 장미가 늦은 봄에
　항상 필 수 있기를 염원하며
살생 중죄와 환경 오염 중죄를 반성하고
과오를 참회하면 평화를 구득

Goldschatz

Confession for Guilt Built by Ignorance of Living Being

Yellow rose implies perfect achievement
Mankind cultures have evolved to achieve perfect convenience
A whale floated down shows its stomach with lots of plastic pieces

To prevent harmful insects pest controls are used each moment
During hunting season many animals are killed by gun science
Dogs or people be killed, which is unconvinced down any times

These days wasps build a hive over a balcony of 17th floor Apt.
My being afraid sprays lots of F-killer to the hive for defense
Wasps coming back gave up the hive, and my peace comes

Ignorance of living being leads to commit all kinds of guilt
These activities harm the earth and people as the effect science
Wasted plastics and global warming incur disasters to societies

Yellow roses would blossom in late Spring till thousand years past
Guilt of killing living beings and polluting acts be deep remorse
The deep remorse on past misconducts brings peaces

장미들의 경쟁을 바라보면서

노랑 장미 종류들은 서로 노랑의 미를 경쟁하고
사람들은 경쟁이라는 이름 아래 남의 아이디어를 훔치며
남의 명의를 도용하여 악업을 쌓는 중죄

음주운전은 나라마다 금지되고
과신하여 음주운전 하면 자/타에게 치명적인 결과를 초래하며
다행히 사고 나지 않으면 요행으로 여기는 중죄

행실 나쁜 죄업으로 가족의 것을 훔치며
품행장애로서 공공의 것을 함부로 파손하고
알게 모르게 부당한 방법으로 재물을 취득하는 중죄

Yellow Simplicity

보이스피싱 범죄는 날로 지능화하며
심약한 사람들은 그들의 덫에 걸려 많은
돈을 뺏기고
그럼에도 개인의 정보는 수없이 그들에게
팔리는 중죄

옐로–심플리시티 장미처럼 아름다움을 서로
경쟁하며
부당한 방법의 경쟁을 싹 쓸어내고
모두가 참회하며 청산해야 할 중죄

Mirroring Rose Competition

Yellow-Simplicity rose competes with other yellow roses
People steal others' idea under the name of competence
Some use somebody's name illegally, which filed up heavy guilt

Drunken driving is prohibited in most countries
Deadly effects incur to others by the cause of over-self-confidence
If an accident does not happen, by chance the luck becomes a deadly habit

Stealing conduct might be started in the families
Conduct disorder caused by frustration could commit vandalism ice
We might commit guilt to get goods unfairly with plans or without

Voice-fishing crimes have evolved intellectually as time goes
The weak-minded got into the trap and lost money as the evidence
Personal info have been sold consistently to the crime conduct

Yellow-Simplicity rose only competes beauty with other roses
Like them we better sweep off all unfair competitions at once
The past unfair crimes must be confessed as the heavy guilt

데이트 품행장애

연노랑 랜도라 장미는 아홉 폭 치마를 두르고
무엇을 숨기고 엷은 미소 지으며
하이라이팅 하네, 사람들의 부도덕한 데이트 중죄

아버지는 젊어서 바람을 피우시고
자녀들은 아버지에 대한 불만을 쌓으며
나이 들면 어머니께 꼼짝 못하고 수난을 받아야 하는 중죄

배우자를 속이고 애인을 사귀며
남의 배우자를 빼앗으려 양심을 버리고
현대인들이 피해야 할 양다리 중죄

Landora

위층과 아래층을 넘나들며 사는 남편도
있으며
같은 동네에 이 집과 저 집을 넘나들며 사는
남편도 있고
언젠가는 들통날 중죄

오늘날 입에 담기 힘든 데이트 중죄가 많으며
이 모든 중죄를 참회하고
용서를 구하며 개과천선해야 할 중죄

Dating Conduct Disorder

Light yellow Landora roses wear nine layer-dress
They smile while hiding something inside
Highlighting the guilt people's immoral dating

There are many having affairs by most fathers
Their children pile up frustration and some try suicide
The guilt incurs aged fathers may get wife's maltreatment waiting

Cheat spouse and have affairs like an ass
They throw away conscience to take other's spouse beside
Modern people are supposed to avoid a double game playing

There are men to come and go upstairs and downstairs as an ass
There are men to live in this house and at the same time another home in a town abode
Soon or later the guilt could be finding

Today there are many cases like having an affair, which shamed to address
Let confess those guilt deeply inside
Let reset the life after asking for forgiving

거짓말은 거짓말을 낳고

꽃대궐 입구를 장식하고 있는 골드-바니 장미가 보이는가?
늑대소년의 눈에는 골드-바니 장미가 예쁘지 않겠는가?
골드-바니 장미는 예쁜 노랑 장미지 않는가?

집안일이 하기 싫어서 숙제가 많다고 거짓말을 해 본 적이 없는가?
임시방편으로 거짓말을 해 본 적이 없는가?
질투 때문에 거짓말을 해 본 적이 없는가?

남의 명예에 흠을 내기 위해 거짓말을 해 본 적이 없는가?
남의 재물을 취하기 위해 거짓말을 해 본 적이 없는가?
나의 허물을 덮기 위해 거짓말을 해 본 적이 없는가?

Gold Bunny

거짓말은 거짓말을 낳음을 모르는가?
사회 구성원으로서 삶에 진실했는가?
오로지 자기 입을 잘 지키기 위해 최선을
다했는가?

가족들에게 거짓말 한 죄를 참회하는가?
이웃과 직장에서 거짓말 한 죄를 참회하는가?
자기 자신에게 거짓말 한 죄를 참회하는가?

Like the Wolf-Boy Lying

Are there Gold Bunny roses decorating an entrance of flower palace
Can't the wolf-boy-liar see Gold Bunny roses are pretty
Gold Bunny roses are pretty yellow, aren't they

Have you ever lied on homework to avoid doing household once
Have you ever lied to avoid a problem at that moment only
Have you ever lied due to jealousy

Have you ever lied to scratch somebody's being famous
Have you ever lied to take somebody's wealth or money
Have you ever lied to cover your fault or saying no sorry

Do you not Know lying yields another lyings
Are you sincere to your life as a member of society
Did you do your best to keep your mouth only

Gold Bunny rose is waiting for your confession at once
Confession on lying to friends, colleagues, and family
Confession on lying to yourself finally

기어(입발림 말)는 신뢰를 깨트리고

골드 파사드 장미에게 "네가 제일 예쁜 장미다"라고 말해 본 적 있는가?
어머니의 꾸중을 피하기 위해 입발림 말해 본 적 있는가?
남의 비위를 맞추기 위해 입발림 말해 본 적 있는가?

잘사는 친척에게 아부해 본 적이 있는가?
잘사는 친구에게 아부해 본 적이 있는가?
직장 상사에게 아부해 본 적이 있는가?

좋은 대우를 받기 위해 아부하고
좋은 평가를 받기 위해 아부하고
빌붙어 살기 위해 아부하고

Gold-Fassade

기어의 대상들은 허상을 만들고
사탕발림 말의 허상은 곧 드러나고
사회적 신뢰는 모래성처럼 언젠가 무너지고

입발림 말 참회하고
아부한 죄 참회하고
동전의 앞면만 말한 죄 참회하고

Buttering up Destroys Trust

Have you ever say to Gold-Fassade rose "You're the most pretty"
To avoid mom's scolding have you ever said "Mom is the best!"
To please somebody have you ever said sweet-word just like that

Have you ever flattered to the rich family
Have you ever flattered to the rich friend like a sycophant
Have you ever flattered to a superior officer at work in front

Butter up to obtain better treat every day
Butter up to receive a good grade on the job assessment
Butter up to mooch with a rich person in and out

The target of being buttered makes virtual image easily
The mirror artifact is revealing itself and soon or later bust
Which destroys every social trust

Let's confess on saying sweet-word without sincerity
Let's confess on buttering up to get benefit
Let's confess on reporting one side of coin and made the other neglect

질투와 시기가 부른 이간계

에밀놀드 장미는 더 돋보이기 위해 이간질을 하지 않고
노란 장미는 질투라는 꽃말을 가지고서도 다투지 않고
돋보이기 위해 각자 멋있게 피고

가족 구성원 간에는 삼각관계가 있고
이웃이나 친척 간에도 삼각관계가 있고
직장 구성원 사이에도 삼각관계가 있고

사람들은 남의 허물을 말하기 좋아하고
제3자에겐 상대의 허물을 말하고
상대와 제3자를 갈라놓고

Emil Nolde

패권을 쥐기 위하여 양설 중죄를 짓고
상대방의 작은 일도 부풀려서 말하고
상대의 편을 갈라치기하고

이간계는 손자병법 중의 하나이고
가족 간에는 손자병법이 필요 없고
노란 장미들 간에도 손자병법은 필요 없고

No Need the Tactic for Yellow Roses Beauty Contest

Emil Nolde roses do not alienate other roses to be outstanding
Yellow roses do not fight although they have meaning of jealousy
They just blossom beautifully to be a best

There might be a triangulation in a family grouping
There might be a triangulation in the neighbors closely
There might be a triangulation in the job sight

People like to talk about their mistakes in order for alienating them
Talking the errors of the other person to the third party intensively
In order to make them separate and against

Report the other party's fault in exaggerating
Commit alienation crime to grasp the hegemony
Make the party into two to make them stand against

Alienating tactic is one of the Art of War
No need the tactic in the family and working harmony
No need the tactic for yellow roses beauty contest

악담, 욕, 저주는 생물의 성장을 저해하고

화이트 크리스마스 장미는 다른 장미들에게 악담하지 않는 하얀 왕
눈처럼 피어 세상의 저주를 씻어 주지
다른 장미들을 욕하지도 않고

SNS 시대에 세상이 싫어 악성 댓글 왕왕
잘나가는 연예인을 인터넷상에서 욕하고 저주하지
그 저주는 어떤 이의 목숨을 잡고

백설공주의 계모는 저주의 대마왕
팥쥐 모녀는 악담의 저수지
동 / 서양 모두 사악한 입을 경고

White Christmas

식물을 키울 때 미소와 덕담을 주면 식물 왕
덕담 받은 식물은 매일 싱싱하게 크지
하물며 꽃들도 그러할진대 동물들은 말할 것도 없고

자아를 개발하는 어린애들도 덕담으로 키우면 지혜의 왕
어린애들은 지혜를 거울삼아 자라지
악담으로 키우면 불행의 씨앗이 되고

Western and Eastern Societies All Are Warning Evil Mouths

White Christmas rose is a king that doesn't have bad mouth
Seeing them itself washes curses of the world
They don't use G Damn words to other roses

There are full of vicious replies due to hate world truth
They curse some hot stars on the internet networking world
The curse takes somebody's life sometimes

The step mom of Snow White was the queen of curse on earth
The mom and Patji were the reservoir of curses in the world
Western and eastern societies all are warning evil mouths

Smile and greetings to plants becomes a green thumb on earth
The plants with warm greetings grow shiny and loud
Not only flowers but pet does

Children with warm encouraging can develop wisdom and faith
They grow older by mirroring wisdom world
If raising with bad mouth, they become seeds of misfortunes

탐심은 범죄를 잉태하고

아이스버그 로즈는 빙산 같은 하얀 눈의 허심
5월을 맑게 노래하는 바른 몸가짐으로 침착
나는 그 뜻을 아는 듯이 학자연

마음이 일으키는 욕심
충족되지 않으면 집착
세상은 내 마음대로만 되지 않고 흘러가는 인연

망상이 초래하는 탐심
나만을 중심으로 카운트하는 분별심의 고착
억지로 성사될 수 없는 망상이 빚어내는 악연

장미를 꺾으려는 탐심
나 혼자만 보겠다는 애착
정작 꺾으려 할 때 가시에 찔리는 우연

욕심부리지 않아도 좋은 이생기심
업의 상속자로서 깨뜨려야 할 집착
탐욕심을 참회하고 또 참회하면 주연

Iceberg

Greediness commits crimes

Iceberg roses show empty mind as the iceberg built by snow
They sing May clearly as if right attitude shows self-possession
I pretend to know their meaning of white scholastically

Mind used to open a greedy window
Unfulfilled greediness opens to the door of obsession
The world affairs go as neglecting one's intention usually

Illusion calls for greediness as a foolish cow
Self-centered counting used to attach to differentiation
Illusion attached to a relationship can't be connected intentionally

Greediness to snap a rose next to the window
Only I can see it with self-centered obsession
One might get pricked by thorns of the rose simultaneously

Empty mind without preconceived notions might be good as much as rainbow
Karma's heritage must be broken not to be born as one's obsession
If being confessed on one's greediness, s / he might be a star finally

성냄과 불만은 왜

마운트-샤스타 장미는 평화롭다
불만도 화냄도 찾아볼 수 없고
아홉 겹 꽃잎으로 웃고 있지 않은가?

내 생각에만 집착하면 화가 난다
어떻게 그럴 수가 있냐고
무엇을 바랬던가?

아무리 생각해도 화가 치민다
세상이 어떻게 이럴 수가 있냐고
입장 바꿔 생각해 봤던가?

Mount Shasta

역지사지 생각해 보면 화는 쪼그라진다
내가 너였더라도 그럴 수 있다고
그러면 서로 민망함은 줄지 않겠는가?

기대에 대한 불만은 화를 키운다
불만스러운 원인을 내게서 찾아보고
다시 시도해 보면 화는 필요 없지 않겠는가?

Angers and Frustrations, Why

Mount-Shasta roses look like peaceful
We cannot find any frustration nor anger in it
They smile with nine layer petals, aren't they

If being obsessed on one's side, s/he feels resentful
How come it goes that way out
What did I expect from the pray

When thinking over and over some must be resentful
Why did it come to happen like that
Have you ever thought the other's situation and what they say

If considering the other's situation, the anger would be crushed awful
If I were you, it could be done that
So each party's embarrassment would be diminished, aren't they

The frustration for expecting would raise being resentful
The frustration factors could be found in my side in fact
If we try it the other way, angers are not necessary, aren't they

이 어리석음은 어찌할꼬

블루문 장미는 예쁘지만 어리석지 않고
보름달이 비추면
그 아름다움은 어디에 숨길꼬

비상식적인 고소득 보장한다는 광고 믿고
수중에 있는 자금 투자하여 날리면
이 어리석음 어찌할꼬

비트코인으로 돈 벌겠다고
빚을 내서 투자한 곳이 어느 날 사라진다면
이 어리석었던 결정 어찌할꼬

Blue Moon

친구 말 듣고
망태 지고 백화점에 쇼핑하러 간다면
이 어리석음 어찌할꼬

이 달콤함이 왜 내게 주어지는가를
　의심해 보고
매 순간마다 조금만 의심해 본다면
생겨나는 지혜는 어찌 좋을꼬

How to Deal with Being Foolish

Blue-Moon roses are pretty but not foolish
When the full Moon rises and lights
Where are they hiding their beautiful attitude

When one trusts an ads saying triple benefits for invests with rush
All the money in hands were invested and lost all in a few nights
How could it be taken care of this foolishness beside

When wanting to earn big fortune by buying Bit-Coin with rush
Although investing with loans to a company it disappears over nights
How to deal with this foolish decision in and out side

Following friends who might be foolish
If s / he goes to a mall in swimming suits
How to take care of this foolish dress code

Let us suspect the sweet offers to us by stopping selfish
If having a little inspection at every moments
How wonderful wisdom comes beside

불교에서의 본래의 나

블루리버 장미도 부처의 본성을 가졌나
연꽃 같은 연보라색이네
밤이면 수월보살이 연못가 블루리버를 찾아오리

본래 부처이나 깨닫지 못하고 있는 나
부처와 나는 둘이 아니라네
마음공부 하다 보면 내 안의 부처 만나게 되리

깨달음의 중요성을 모르는 중생에게는 선과 악을 방편으로 이끄나
다음 단계는 욕심과 집착을 내려놓는 방편을 설하시네
본론은 이 세상은 하나의 꿈이니 깨어나리

부처는 차별 없는 무한한 자비심을 가지나
인과응보는 있다네
깨닫기 전에 지은 인과는 깨달은 후에도 남으리

Blue River

법문을 들으면 내 안의 본래 부처가 듣다가 어느 찰나
내 안의 부처가 법문을 공명할 때에 깨달음이 일어나네
일순간에 깨닫게 되리

꽃을 보고도 그 공명이 일어날 수 있기도 하나
까마귀 소리 듣다가 깨달음이 일어날 수 있다네
부처는 새벽 별을 보고 깨달으셨으니 그 언제를
어찌 알리

Original Me in the Buddhism

Blue-River roses might have a Buddha's nature
They have light purple color like lotus
At night Suwal Bosal might visit Blue-River roses next the pond

I am not aware that I was originally a Buddha before
The Buddha and me are not two different natures
I might meet the Buddha in me while practicing studying of mind

Leads mankind neglecting the gravity of enlightenment with good-evil measure
Next level explains the tactics to put down obsession and greediness
The core is one's awakening from a dream of this world

Buddha shows unlimited mercies without discrimination as the core
However the nature asks cause and effect laws
The cause before enlightening takes the effect after being enlightened

When listening to the Buddha words a Buddha in me could be aware
An enlightenment rises when a Buddha in me causes resonance to the Words
At a moment the enlightenment might be happened

The resonance might be appeared by watching flower without a lecture
The resonance might be appeared by hearing cawing of crows
The Buddha got enlightenment by watching dawn stars, so we never know when it be appeared

참회와 수행의 본질

여기저기 마르졸렌 장미가 활짝 피듯이 우리 죄 무성하니
이제 우리는 신업, 구업, 의업 등 무성한 죄업을 참회하고
이제 죄업의 근원을 다스려야 하고

오랜 세월 쌓인 죄업 참회하고 수행하니
큰 깨달음의 한 찰나에 없어지고
마른 풀이 타버리듯 남김없이 사라지고

죄는 본래 스스로 반성함이 없어서 마음 따라 일어나니
죄를 짓는 마음이 사라지면 죄도 함께 없어지고
꿈같은 마음조차 없이 하는 마음공부는 진실한 참회라고

Marjolaine

욕심과 집착을 내려놓으니
허망한 꿈은 사라지고
죄를 짓는 마음도 사라지고

마음공부를 수행하니
죄와 마음이 공해지고
그것이 진실한 참회라고

The Core of Confession

Our guilt blossom as Marjolaine roses blossomed fully here and there
Now we confess the guilt by conduct, speaking, and mind
Now we need to deal with the core of guilt clearly

The guilt piled up for long time must be confessed and mindful practice here
A big enlightenment wipes it out at a moment or second
As dried grasses were burnt it disappears thoroughly

The guilt rises according to mind without self-reflection as a core
The guilt is disappeared if the crime mind itself is disappeared
The real confession is to practice mind without illusion absolutely

By putting down greediness and obsession right here
As the illusion is disappeared
The mind for crime is also disappeared apparently

By cultivating mindful practice as the Buddha core
The guilt and mind are emptied
That is a real confession genuinely

참회의 진언으로 내 안의 부처를 찾고

사이운 장미는 주홍색 장미이기에
첫사랑의 고백이라는 꽃말을 가지고
손꼽아 고백에 대한 답을 기다리리

내 안에 본래 부처 있기에
처음의 부처는 법문을 듣다 어느 순간 깨닫게 되고
본래의 답은 법문 너머에 진실로 깨달음으로 오리

Saiun

의미와 의식 너머에
나를 이끄는 참회 진언을 끊임없이 독송하고
일체 불보살께 귀의하리

옴 살바못자 모지 사다야 사바하
옴 살바못자 모지 사다야 사바하
옴 살바못자 모지 사다야 사바하

내가 본래 부처이기에
본래대로 돌아가겠다고
본래의 나로 돌아가리

Buddha as the Original Core in Me

Saiun roses are scarlet color
The color meaning implies the first love confession
Waiting for the answer for the propose

Because a Buddha resides in me as the original color
At a moment I get enlightened while listening to Buddha speech session
There be a real enlightenment beyond speeches and sutras or else

Beyond meaning and consciousness director
Ceaselessly reciting the phrases of confession
Devoted to all of Buddha Bosals leading mercy and being concise

Oum Salbamotja Moji Sadaya Sabaha
Oum Salbamotja Moji Sadaya Sabaha
Oum Salbamotja Moji Sadaya Sabaha

Because I am a Buddha as nature as the original core color
I will come back to the original station
Come back to my original sense

준제 관세음보살께 귀의

Love Ⅱ 장미는 또 다른 주홍색이어라
주홍색 장미의 꽃말 중에는 수줍음이 있고
종국에는 순수한 솔직함 되도록

인간계의 중생을 사랑으로 구제하는 관음이어라
자비심으로 모든 장애와 괴로움에서 벗어나도록 돕고
종국에는 깨달음으로 성불하도록

준제 관세음보살은 모든 공덕을 닦아 얻는 복덕과 지혜의 보고이어라
고요한 마음으로 항상 준제진언을 외우고
종국에는 이 세상 온갖 재난이 침범하지 못하도록

하늘이나 사람이나 모든 중생을 구제하리라
부처님과 다름없는 복을 받고
이 같은 부처의 본성을 지니는 이가 되도록

Love Ⅱ

불성을 찾은 이는 결정코 최상의 법 이루리라
칠억 명의 부처를 키워 낸 부처의 어머니께
　귀의하고
귀의하고 또 귀의하도록

나무 칠구지 불모 대준제보살
나무 칠구지 불모 대준제보살
나무 칠구지 불모 대준제보살

Devote to the Junje Gwan Seum Bosal

Love II American roses have another scarlet beauty
The scarlet rose implies a shyness
Finally being shy is a pure and honest expression

Junje Bosal is a Goddess of Mercy to aide mankind difficulty
Helps to get out all barriers and hardships
Finally leads to be a Buddha with getting enlightened situation

The Bosal is a reservoir of wisdom and rewards of virtue
Always recites Junje Wish Phrases with calm mind perhaps
Finally to make that all world disasters should not become violation

Save all mankind, human, or heaven in safety
Receive the same fortune as the Buddha speaks
To become whom obtains this Buddha's nature

The one finding the Buddha nature will achieve the highest law-authority
Devote to the mother of the Buddha who raised 700,000,000 ones
Devote and dedicate humble devotion

Namu chilguji Bulmo Dae Junje Bosal
Namu chilguji Bulmo Dae Junje Bosal
Namu chilguji Bulmo Dae Junje Bosal

깨달음을 얻기 위한 방편으로서의 진언들

마갈리 장미는 수줍게 우리를 바라보고
진언의 방편으로 기도하기를 바라고
이 진언들로 생각 너머의 나를 찾아 나섬

정법계 진언으로서 청정한 법계는 마음을 맑게 하고
법계를 맑게 하는 진언은 마음을 모으게 하고
옴남, 옴남, 옴남

호신진언은 몸을 보호하게 하고
탐심, 화냄, 어리석음으로부터 보호하고
옴 치림, 옴 치림, 옴 치림

관세음보살의 미묘한 본마음을 보여주고
여섯 자의 대명왕 진언은 진언 중 최고이고
옴 마니 반메홈, 옴 마니 반메홈, 옴 마니 반메홈

Magali

준제진언은 7억 명의 부처님께 귀의하고
준제보살께서 설하옵고
나무 사다남 삼먁 삼못다 구차남 다녀타

옴 자례주례 준제 사바하 부림
옴 자례주례 준제 사바하 부림
옴 자례주례 준제 사바하 부림

The Praying Words Beyond Thinking to Get Enlightened

Shy Magali rose looks at you
Asks you to pray with tactics of true words
These words lead us to find 'me' beyond thinking aim

The words to clear law world cleans our mind plateau
To concentrate and purify our minds
Om Nam Om Nam Om Nam

Self-protection Words let all attacks adieu
Protect us from greediness, angers, and foolish minds
Om Chirim Om Chirim Om Chirim

By showing the mysterious original mind of the Gwan Seum Bosal to thou
The six letters of DaeMyoung Wang Words is the best words
Om Mani Banmeom, Om Mani Banmeom, Om Mani Banmeom

The Junje Words pray to devote to the 700,000,000 Buddha for you
The Junje Bosal gives the praying beyond meaning of words
Namu Sadanam Sammak Sammotda Guchanam Danyouta

Om Jaryejurye Junje Sabaha Burim
Om Jaryejurye Junje Sabaha Burim
Om Jaryejurye Junje Sabaha Burim

준제 보살의 발원

Montparsas 장미가 환하게 노래하니
첫사랑도 수줍음도 뒤로 하고
평안한 마음과 깨달음을 추구하네

이제 준제주를 지극히 부르오니
준제 관세음보살께 발원하고
크나크신 준제를 칭송하네

준제 관세음보살께서는 인간계를 구제하시니
보리심을 발하시고
큰 소원을 세우시네

번뇌 사라지게 하시니
있는 그대로를 통찰하시고
이 마음 어서 속히 밝아지게 하시네

Montparsas

모든 복덕과 지혜를 남김없이 성취하게
　하시니
특히 뛰어난 복을 두루두루 장엄하시고
모든 중생들의 깨달음이 이뤄지게 하시네

Offering the Junje Bosal's Pray

Montparsas roses smile happily
Putting back the first love and shyness
Pursuits a comfortable mind and enlightenment

Now calls the Junje Bosal vitally
Praying for the Junje Gwan Seum Bosal as an avatar of the Goddess
Praises the Junje as the greatest

The Junje Bosal aids the human world especially
Spreads out aspiration for Buddhahood everywhere it needs
Sets up wishes as the greatest

The Junje Bosal makes the agonies disappear finally
Observes thoroughly as it is
Makes this mind very quickly bright

The Bosal makes practicing good deeds achieve rewards thoroughly
Especially manages outstanding fortunes in any directions
Let all mankind achieve an enlightenment

부처님께 드리는 열 가지 기도

프라그란트-레이디 장미는 핑크의 우아한 근원
행복한 사랑의 꽃말을 가지고
욕심, 성냄, 어리석음을 버리고서

내 마음 속의 욕심, 성냄, 어리석음은 죄의 근원
원하오니 이 셋을 영원히 버리고
그 삼독심을 속히 끊고서

좋은 공부 함께 하는 것은 마음공부의 근원
내 주변의 불법승이 학교를 이루고
불법승 삼보 말씀을 항상 듣고서

좋은 말씀을 지키고 분별심을 버리는 불원
삼악도를 힘써 닦아내고
부처님을 따라서 항상 마음챙김 배우고서

Fragrant Lady

원컨대 보리심에 항상 머무는 본원
결정코 깨달음의 세계에 가서 다시 태어나고
내가 바로 부처의 자리에 돌아오고서

아미타불 부처님을 친견하는 소원
온 세계 모든 중생이 깨달음을 얻고
모든 중생 빠짐없이 건져지는 발원서

The Praying Statement to the Buddha

Fragrant Lady rose is the base of pink as young girls like best
The pink rose meaning implies a happy love for good
Throws away greediness, anger, and foolishness as well

The greediness, anger, and foolishness in my mind is the base of guilt
Please let us throw the three evil minds for good
Please let us cut quickly the three kinds of evil minds all

Studying together is the base of mind practice as Buddhist
Buddha, sutra, and monks around me make a mindful wood
And always listen to Buddha, sutra, and monks well

Buddhist base asks to keep rules and cut discriminating mind set
Practice to cut the three kinds of evil minds in deed
Study always to follow the Buddha mindful

Stay in the base of aspiration for Buddhahood as wishing most
Definitely get a rebirth in the enlightenment world
So I come back to the very Buddha place well

The wish for meeting the Amitabul Buddha at last
Enlightenment comes to every mankind in the world
This is the praying statement to save every mankind at all

네 가지 큰 바램

퀸-엘리자베스 장미는 분홍으로 분홍 하여
위 없는 분홍으로 피우오리다
분홍장미의 여제

먼저 마음챙김으로 나를 구제하여
가없는 중생을 건져오리다
마음챙김으로 주변을 도우면 일체중생도 구제

생각의 번뇌는 끝없이 꼬여
끝없는 번뇌를 끊어오리다
내 안의 번뇌를 끊어서 꼬여진 눈앞을 구제

Queen-Elizabeth

마음챙김으로 수련하여
한없는 법문을 배우오리다
내 안의 법문을 익혀서 있는 그대로
보는 체제

법문을 듣고 깨달음을 성취하여
위 없는 불도를 이루오리다
내 안의 불도를 이루어 마음챙김의 축제

The Four Wishes

Queen-Elizabeth rose does shine as pink really
It blossoms as pink as the best
Queen of all kinds of pink roses

Mindfulness aids me firstly
It would help me to aid mankind without limit
If helping neighbors with mindfulness, we could aid all human beings

Thinking of agonies harasses endlessly
By cutting agonies in my mind
Cut off the troubles inside me and relieve my twisted realities in front of eyes

Practice mindfully
Study and listen to all speeches on the Buddha teaching text
By appreciating the speeches in me let us see the world as it self

Achieve enlightenment by listening to the teachings of Buddha sincerely
Achieve the Buddhist doctrines to the top of height
The doctrines in my mind enjoys mindful festivals

삼보께 귀의

Pink Peace

핑크 피스 장미는 세 가지 특징이 있지
색깔이 분홍이며
정말로 핫-핑크지

핑크 피스 장미는 평화라는 뜻도 있지
가시를 가지고 있지만 평화로우며
그 자체로서 예쁜 장미지

불교에는 세 가지 보물이 있지
먼저 불교의 근원인 부처님이 계시며
어디에든지 계시지

불교는 부처님 가르침이 2500년간 면면히 흐르지
내 안의 부처를 마음챙김으로 찾으라 하시며
각자의 깨달음으로 모든 중생을 도우라 하시지

부처님의 가르침은 출세간에 계신 스님들께서 전하시지
부처님 가르침을 수행과 경전 공부로 터득하시며
세간의 중생들을 법문으로 깨우치시지

늘 계시는 시방의 모든 부처님께 귀의하고 받드옵니다
늘 계시는 시방의 모든 가르침에 귀의하고 받드옵니다
늘 계시는 시방의 모든 사부대중께 귀의하고 받드옵니다

The Three Treasures

The pink-peace roses have three aspects literally
The color is pink
It is hot pink really

The pink-peace rose has 'peace' in it naturally
In spite of having thorns it says peace pink
It is a pretty rose it self really

Buddhism has three treasures systemically
Firstly there is Buddha as the think-tank
Buddha says Buddha exists everywhere evenly

The teaching has taught mankind for 2500 years world widely
Aids mankind to find ones Buddha in them by mindful think–tank
Asks to aid all mankind by obtaining enlightenment mindfully

Monks in temples let mankind know Buddha's teaching practically
The teaching is told through undergoing disciplines by every monk
Monks lead mankind to find a Buddha mindfully

So devote to Buddha existing everywhere world widely
Devote to all the teaching of Buddha in each book
Devote to all the monks everywhere world widely

몸, 입, 뜻을 깨끗하게 하는 기도

Esmeralda 분홍장미는 대찬 줄기, 깨끗한 잎들, 고운 꽃봉오리
대찬 줄기는 깨끗한 잎들을 뻗고
꽃봉오리는 Edge 있게

아침이슬 사라진 낮에도 분홍이 맑게 빛나는 꽃봉오리
잎들은 싱싱하게 햇빛을 받고
줄기는 하늘 향해 대차게

관세음보살의 자비를 받는 자들은 몸, 입, 뜻이 깨끗하리
이 세상 모든 법은 본성이 원래 청정하고
훌륭한 것이므로 일체 만법이 청정하게

Esmeralda

우리 자신 또한 이 법과 더불어 청정해지리
그렇게 될 때 행동, 말, 뜻도 깨끗하게 되고
마음챙김으로 행동, 말, 뜻을 항상 깨끗하게

옴 사바바바 수다살바 달마 사바바바 수도함
옴 사바바바 수다살바 달마 사바바바 수도함
옴 사바바바 수다살바 달마 사바바바 수도함

Pray for Cleaning Body, Mouth, and Intention

Esmeralda roses have strong stems, clean leafs, and clear pink buds
Strong stem stretches clean leafs forth
Each clear pink bud shows clear edges together

Although morning dew disappeared it shows shiny pink buds
Leafs are fresh with sunshine on the earth
Stems stretch toward the sky stronger

Ones with mercy from Gwan-Seum-Bosal have clean mouths and bodies
The nature of all orders is clean and clear on the earth
They are great so that all the orders are clearer and cleaner

We are also clean and clear like the orders
When it does so, our acts, words, and intentions are clean worth
With mindfulness the threesome are clearer and cleaner

Om Sabababa Sudasalba Dalma Sabababa Sudoham
Om Sabababa Sudasalba Dalma Sabababa Sudoham
Om Sabababa Sudasalba Dalma Sabababa Sudoham

기도 법단을 여는 진언

프루이트 장미는 오렌지색에 주홍이 야단법석을 떨며
바람개비와 같은 마음가짐
새로운 장르의 오렌지 핑크가 열리네

프루이트 장미는 함박 웃으며
여기저기 소망의 마음가짐
복스럽게 다닥다닥 열리네

마당에서 기도할 단을 열고 법석을 마련하며
부처님께 기도할 그러한 마음가짐
금강의 문이 열리네

그 속에서 어떤 일심으로 정진하며
그런 삼매의 분위기 가짐
우리 모두 두루두루 경건한 일심으로 들어가네

Fruite

옴 바아라 놔로 다가다야 삼마야 바라제
사야훔
옴 바아라 놔로 다가다야 삼마야 바라제
사야훔
옴 바아라 놔로 다가다야 삼마야 바라제
사야훔

The Pray to Prepare Praying Place

Fruite roses make a fuss with coloring scarlet
Showing mindset like a pinwheel
It opens a new genre of orange pink rose

Fruite roses are smiling burst
Wishing mindset blossom here and there all
Happily hanging in close

In the yard to make a praying place with a table set
With praying mindset to Buddha as Amitabul
While making a fuss, the Diamond Door opens

In the happy fuss everyone devotes oneself as a mind-set
Absorption samadhi atmosphere is built as a whole
All of us go back to a holy mind without exceptions

Om Baahra Nwaro Dagadaya Sammaya Baraje Saya Hum
Om Baahra Nwaro Dagadaya Sammaya Baraje Saya Hum
Om Baahra Nwaro Dagadaya Sammaya Baraje Saya Hum

기도 법단을 세우는 진언

Concertino 주홍 장미가 예사롭지 않게 기쁘게 웃고
나도 장미라고 구획을 세우고
또 다른 특색의 장미를 기도하는 낙원으로

단을 세우면서 단을 만들고
기쁘게 단을 세우고
그래서 법희 선열의 낙원으로

기도 분위기 유지가 되도록 해 주시고
불단을 세우고
부처님과 보살들을 청해서 모심으로

의식을 집행하려고 준비하고
기뻐서 야단법석을 떨고
삶은 우리 눈앞에 기쁨과 환희의 분위기로

옴 난다난다 나지나지 난다바리 사바하
옴 난다난다 나지나지 난다바리 사바하
옴 난다난다 나지나지 난다바리 사바하

Concertino

The Pray for Setting the Table to Pray

Concertino scarlet roses smile with especial pleasure
They are also a kind of rose and occupy a part of the rose garden
Decorate and pray another special rose paradise

At the praying place monks set up the praying table there
With pleasure the table is set in the clean and clear garden
So it becomes a paradise of Buddha teaching and Mercy Goddess

The enlightenment let it be a praying atmosphere
Monks set a sitting table for Buddha in the garden
Making a fuss to prepare a pray for Buddhahood with being please

To prepare the praying ceremony there
Everyone with dazzling smile makes a fuss calmly in the garden
Making a fuss is enjoying full of delight paradise

Om Nandananda Najinaji Nandabari Sabaha
Om Nandananda Najinaji Nandabari Sabaha
Om Nandananda Najinaji Nandabari Sabaha

법의 세계를 깨끗이 하는 진언

Monica 주홍 장미는 챙 넓은 모자에 꽂기에 예쁘다
납작하게 환히 피어서 좋고
모자에 값진 장식과도 같이 뚜렷하다

깨끗한 삶을 색으로 보면 텅 비어서 깨끗하고 맑다
글자로 보면 공의 점으로써 장엄하고
그 모양이 상투 위에 값진 구슬을 올려놓은 것같이 뚜렷하다

그 나 자의 정상에다 딱 둠으로 '남' 자가 된다
그래서 진언이 법계와 하나가 되고
그 진언은 한량없는 죄를 소멸케 한다

Monica

'남'은 지혜의 불로 모든 죄를 다 태워 버린다
이렇게 해서 지혜의 불로써 우리의 번뇌를 몰아내고
세상을 환하게 밝혔을 때 그때 삶의 세계가 청정해
진다

나무 사만다 못다남 남
나무 사만다 못다남 남
나무 사만다 못다남 남

The Pray for Cleaning the World of Living

Monica scarlet rose is a good ornament for a wide-brimmed hat
It is appropriate to decorate for the hat by a bit flat blossoming
It looks like a precious ornament for a hat clearly

Pure life is clear and clean if being expressed in color concept
The formation with a dot on it is magnificent in literally looking
It looks like a topknot with a precious pearl on it clearly

'Nam' means a best word by putting a top on a Buddhism concept
So the praying words coincides with the same as the world of Buddhist living
'Nam' makes the limitless guilt disappear purely

'Nam' as the fire of wisdom burns all the guilt
The fire of wisdom throws away our agonies and suffering
When all of them disappeared the living world becomes clean clearly

Namu Samanda Motdanam Nam
Namu Samanda Motdanam Nam
Namu Samanda Motdanam Nam

Part II

산사의 꽃수들
Temple Flower Fancy Works of Mind

발우와 길거리 공연

세존은 외향형이 아니셨을까
발우 들고 걸식어기성중(乞食於其城中) 하시니
내향형 스님은 그 옛날엔 어찌 공양 하셨을까

봉황산 부석사는 숲속 오르막에 지었을까
층층이 법당을 지으니
눈 덮인 산사에 미끄럽지는 않았을까

신라 676년 화엄종 근본도량의 대교는 달랐을까
절을 짓기 위해 선묘 신룡이 바위를 들어 올리니
부석으로 불려 무량수전 뜰 아래 석룡 되어 묻혔을까

게일은 산사 부근을 맴돌며 노래하였을까
뒤늦게 노래에 매료되니
하라는 공부는 제쳐두고 노래하러 다녔을까

발우나 길거리 공연은 어떻게 같을까
무림의 산사에 꽃을 담당하니
노래로 꽃들을 길렀을까

Alms Food and Busking

Was the Buddha extrovert
With his bowel to seek alms food in the great city
How did introvert monks seek his alms in the city

Why was Buseoksa temple at the Bongwhangsan uphill built
Each Buddha hall was built at each hill
Was not slippery the snow-covered temple hill

In 676, Was the fundamental principles of the Whaeum Order different
To build halls, a miraculous dragon carried big rocks upon the hill yard
It was called Buseok burried under Muryangsujeon yard after its dead

Did Gael walk and sing around the Temple hills
He was charmed by singing songs in twenties
Did he go busking Instead of studying for midterm exams

How are similar between alms food and busking
Looks like taking a role of temple flower fancy working
Did he raise flowers by singing

선(善)은 선(禪)을 통하여

어떻게 선(善)을 쌓아야 하는지 세존께 여쭈니
아뇩다라삼막삼을 얻으려는 보리심을 발하고
그에 머물며 그 마음을 펼쳐야 한다고

금정(金井)산 큰 바위 샘물에 금빛 물고기 노니니
산기슭에 범어사(梵魚寺) 짓고
수행자와 민초들의 의지 역할을 하고

신라 678년 화엄종의 큰 사찰 이루니
영남의 3대 사찰의 위상을 지니고
1910년 선원 개설 후 선 수행의 중심도량이 되고

선(善)은 선(禪)을 통하여 자신과 싸워 터득하니
외향적인 대니는 금정산성에 올라 노래하고
숯불 피워 일일 급식하고

금정총림의 선원이 위상을 떨치니
호기심 많은 대니는 산사를 관찰하고
수많은 암자의 꽃들을 노래하고

The Good Is Grasped by Meditation

Ask Buddha how to practice the good
The answer was to emanate mercy mind to obtain enlightenment
Stay there and spread out the mind

In a rock-spring of the Mt. Geumjeong there was a fish in gold
To celebrate this, on the hillside the miracle fish temple was built
The temple plays a religious role of devoting monks and mankind

The temple became a biggest Whaeum Party in 678 Silla dynasty indeed
The status was one of three best temples in the southeast
In 1910 it opened a meditation center that keyed to practice mind

The good is grasped by meditating and getting over ones agony mind
Danny climbed the Mt. hills to avoid agony and sang like an extrovert
He was working at a restaurant by making fires to cook food

The meditation center got famous as the main temple of meditating mind
Curious Danny wishing to be a singer observed the temple hills sight
He kept singing winter flowers at small temples in the Mt. around

아인중생수자(我人衆生壽者)에의 집착

대승정종(大乘正宗)은 중생을 무여열반으로 제도하도록
사실은 제도 받은 중생은 없으며
아인중생수자(我人衆生壽者) 등의 상은 보살이 아니라고

비로암은 통일신라 시대의 비로자나불 보고 깨닫도록
깨달음과 어리석음이 하나라고 손으로 가르치시며
우리의 본래 부처였음과 깨달음이 공존함을 강조하고

대방광불화엄경 일곱 자는 마음 심 한 자로 깨치도록
선용기심(善用其心) 생겨야 하며
각자 마음을 잘 써 평온과 성취를 이루라고

이상주의적인 스탠은 마음을 잘 쓰도록
산사를 돌면서 시를 쓰며
눈 덮인 팔공산 바라보며 몇 가락 읊조리고

스탠은 사람들을 이해하고 글로 표현하도록
글재주를 개발하며
꽃과 아인중생수자의 상을 노래하고

Obsessing to Oneself, Others, Mankind, and Life

The great Buddhism party leads all mankind to enter nirvana
If everyone is already a Buddha, so no one was leaded by the effort
Obsessing to oneself, others, mankind, and life is not Buddha's mind

Biroam temple was built in the Silla to enlighten like the Birojana Buddha
The finger pointing form says it is one that ignorant mind is enlightenment
Emphasizing we are simultaneously being of Buddha and enlightened

To understand a word 'mind' is a core of the seven letter sutra
Must generate the mind of using good will every moment
Requesting each uses ones mind well to get peace and being achieved

An idealist Stan wanted to use his mind well walla
Writing poems while walking around the temple on the mount
Intones a few lines while watching the Mt. Palgongsan snowed

Stan expresses literally his understanding people around the area
Develops his writing talent
Chants flowers and the images of oneself, others, life, and mankind

상(相)에 머물지 않는 보시

세존께서 보시를 하되 상(相)에 머물지 말라시네
색(눈에 보이는 세상)에 머물지 아니하며
소리, 향기, 맛에 의해 깨닫지 말라시네

김영한은 진향, 자야, 길상화로 불렸다네
대원각을 바쳐서 길상사를 창건하며
무주상보시(상에 머물지 않는 보시) 하네

법정스님의 무소유를 몸소 실천하였다네
끝내 놓지 못한 허상은 백석 되며
육신의 옷 벗을 때 눈 오는 날 길상현 뜰에 뿌려달라네

잘 나가던 진(Jean)은 청중이 두려웠다네
떨림으로 외로움으로 괴로워하며
어느새 노래를 마칠 수 없었다네

상(相)에 머물지 않는 보시의 유래를 미처 몰랐었네
진(Jean)은 대성각에서 도태하며
극복은 외부가 아니라 내 마음에서 찾아야 하네

Doing Mercy That Does Not Stay at Thinking Images

Buddha tells not to stay at thinking images when doing mercy
Not to stay at the world you see
Not to judge according to sound, scent, and taste

Kim, Younghan was called Real-Scent, Jaya, or Kilsang-Flower in a way
She donated her restaurant park to build the Kilsang temple
Her donating mercy was not to stay at thinking images as private

She fulfilled the 'nonpossession' of Monk Beobjeong personally
But the illusion she did not let go became the White-rock finale
Asked to sprinkle her ashes on the backyard of the temple in snow white

Jean with some fame got afraid of his audience one day
Agony gave him loneliness with suffering to see
Could not finish his singing note

He did not know the Kilsangsa temple history
Jean fell behind at the restaurant park there
Overcoming is supposed to find guts inside not from out state

실다운 진실을 보라

눈에 보이는 형상으로 여래를 볼 수 있는가
실다운 진실을 보라
진리는 우리가 보고 있는 것이 다가 아님을

신라 헌강왕이 방문하여 실다운 진실을 보라라 하였던가
도선국사의 877년 창건 당시를 보라
국사께서도 눈에 보인 것에 머무셨음을

왕께서도 법에 머물러 보시하셨던가
왕산사라 칭하지 않았다면 그 복덕을 헤아리지 못하리라
응당 가르친 바와 같이 머물라 하셨음을

인정 많고 내향적인 빌(Bill)은 법에 머물렀던가
성실하게 땀 흘려 역사함을 보라
틈틈이 기도하며 힘을 키우려 했음을

한겨울에 빌은 뼈를 다치고
주저앉았던가
수려한 왕방산의 기를 보라
청아한 목소리로 노동요를 불렀음을

Look at the Real Fact

Can we see the Buddha as the real image tactically
Look at the real fact
The truth we can see is not everything

Named the Wongsansa due to the King Heongang's visiting loyally
Look at that time of the temple in 877 when a great monk Dosun built
Monk Dosun stayed at an image that he saw the King meant in Korean wong

Did the King donate mercy to the temple by staying at images vastly
The reward of virtue could have been uncountable if other naming it
Buddha says not to stay at what you are seeing

Did warmhearted Bill stay at the images introversively
Look at his diligence and working energy in wet
He tried to raise power while time to time praying

Did Bill break bones in winter and give up his talent naturally
Look at the spirit of the Wongbangsan mount
In clear ringing voice he sang for working

한 생각이나마 신뢰하는 마음

세존의 장구한 언설은 여래 입적 후 2500년이 지나도
한 생각이나마 신뢰하는 마음을 지니게 되느니
여래는 중생이 무량복덕을 얻고자 함을 아심이라

보문산 촛대바위 품어 고촉사라는 이름도
대적광전 옆 석조여래좌상은 중생에게 시무외인(施無畏印) 하시니
중생의 무량복덕 도우심이라

아인중생수자* 없어지면 법상도
비법상도 다 없어지니
옳은 법을 취하더라도 상을 취하면 아인중생수자에 집착하게 됨이라

외향적인 개빈은 객관적이기도
아인중생수자에 집착하지 않겠노라니
탈놀이와 광대 패에도 넘나듦이라

목소리는 고촉사 범종 소리만큼 높고도
아름답고 청아하니
어느 한쪽 청중이라도 신뢰함이라

* 아인중생수자: 我相('나'라는 생각), 人相(남이라는 차별의식), 衆生相(중생이라는 열등의식), 壽者相(목숨이라는 한계의식)

Trust at Least a Thought

The Buddha's long long speeches still exist after he died 2500 years ago
Because one can trust at least a thought Buddha explained
Buddha knows mankind want to get endless rewards of virtue

Seeing a candle rock in the Mt. led to the name Gochok(high candle)sa
The stone Buddha hold up five fingers to remove fears from mankind
Helps mankind obtain limitless rewards of virtue

As the images of self, others, and etc disappear, images of right law do so
The images of wrong law also disappeared
Although taking right laws and having images, which led to self, others, and etc image

Extrovert Gavin is nonpartisan also
Not to addict to self, others, life, and mankind
He is in and out playing entertainer and mask parade

His voice is high like the temple bell of the Gochoksa and tune like cello
The beautiful and clear ringing voice he had
Might be any part of audiences trusting his voice

진화의 수천 년의 원리

여래께서 아뇩다라삼막삼보리*를 얻지 않으셨고
이는 고정된 법이 없는 것 자체를 이름함이며
여래는 인류 진화의 수천 년의 원리를 내다보심이라

모두 취할 수도 설할 수도 없고
그 이후의 현자들께서는 시대를 초월하여 내다보며
그러한 고정되지 않은 이치를 상대적으로 설하심이라

832년(신라 흥덕 7년) 심지왕사가 창건하고
겨울 절 주위에 오동나무꽃 만발하여 동화사라 명명하며
선 / 교 / 율 통하여 아뇩다라삼막삼보리를 실천하심이라

외향적인 책은 목청 높여 읊조리고
왁자지껄 '당기시오'를 외치며
무득무설(無得無說)에 대해서는 무관심이라

높디높은 목소리는 팔공산에 닿고
오동나무꽃 자주 꽃 겨울 산 바라보며
목청을 연마함이라

* 아뇩다라삼막삼보리: 가장 높고 바른 깨달음

The Principle Human Being Has Evolved Thousands Years

Buddha did not obtain the enlightenment, Anyokdarasammaksambory
Which means there is no fixed way itself
Buddha realized the principle human being has evolved thousands years

Cannot be taken all nor explained everything picky
Sages after Buddha could also see the future beyond the times
They explained the unfixed principle relatively as it applies also nowdays

Monk Simji built the Dongwhasa temple in 832 in Silla dynasty
Dongwha means 'winter flowers' blossomed on royal foxglove trees roof
To get enlighten monks practiced meditation, teaching, and Buddhist rules

Extrovert Jack recited songs loudly
Shouting 'pull in' boisterous sound stuff
Ignorant about 'no gain, no explain' of Buddha teachings

His high and loud voice reached to the Mt. Palgongsan valley
Watching the violet flowers of the trees and the snowy mount itself
Was for practicing his voice of great compass

보시보다 큰 복덕

삼천 대천 세계 칠보를 보시하더라도
즉시 그 복덕을 받을 수 없으며
복덕도 아니라 하시네

여래 말씀 중에서 사구게*등을 수지하고도
남들에게 설명해 주며
그 복덕은 보시보다 크다 하시네

신라 문무왕 때 명랑대사가 창건한 사찰이고도
통도사 말사로서 여래 경전과 사구게를 전하며
임진왜란 시 승병 모아 맞서 싸워서 호국하였네

이안은 어사화는 쓰지 못하고도
응진전 내부천정의 화려한 단청처럼 돋보이며
어사화 회화나무는 이미 400세가 넘었다네

먼 훗날의 복덕 바라보면서도
붙임성 있고 품위 있으며
함월산 산사 돌며 노래하네

* 사구게: 금강경의 핵심사상을 간략한 4구의 형식으로 나타낸 게송

Reward of Virtue That Is Bigger Than Treasure Donation

Although you donate world treasures gathering over three oceans
You may not get the reward of virtue immediately
Buddha says it may not be even a qualification for a reward of virtue

While learning and achieving the Buddha teachings
You share and explain the Buddha teachings to others widely
This reward of virtue is bigger than the treasure donation virtue

Monk Myoungrang built the temple in the Silla dynasty times
An affiliated temple to the Tongdosa has spread the teachings continuously
In the Imjin war patriotic monks fought against Japan to rescue

Ian could not wear a royal embassy hat with flowers
Outstanding like the ceiling's showy patterns of Eungjinjeon hall holy
While the flower tree is over 400 years old with a great value

He tried to raise a hope to obtain the hat with flowers as rewards
While maintaining sociability and behavior dignity moderately
Singing around the Hamwalsan mount until being fatigue

중생은 본래 없는 것

중생은 본래 없는 것이므로
중생이 성불할 수 없다 하시니
부처가 일왕래(一往來)하여 부처 되신다

도선사는 862년 신라(경문왕) 도선국사가 창건하므로
일천년 내다보며 지으니
그때 말법(末法)시대 예견하시다

이 시대는 실로 그때와 무한대로 다르므로
예견하신 대로 말법이라 할 수 있으니
일상무상(一相無相)을 즐기기 어렵다

걸쭉하나 가창력 뛰어나므로
말법시대에도 눈에 띄이니
공양간에서도 데일은 수행한다

공양 짓다 공부하므로
한눈에도 법당에 수행하는 자가 많으니
남과 비교되는 내가 걱정이다

Mankind Did not Exist Originally

Because mankind did not exist originally
Buddha says mankind cannot be a Buddha
Just each Buddha comes and goes as a birth in the world

Because Monk Doseon built the Doseonsa temple in 862 originally
He could spread his perspective over hundreds of era
Still the troubled era is continued

Although this era became so different from that times really
As he predicted this world looks like a troubled era
It is rare to enjoy the Buddha saying everyday is not to be obsessed

His singing ability is outstanding like his height highly
His ability is caught by the neighbors' eyes in this era
In the temple kitchen Dale practiced

Because he practices while cooking rice diligently
There are so many disciplinants in the temple hall reciting Buddha
Comparing to others "I am worried"

불토(佛土)의 장엄은 장엄이 아니라고

중생을 구제키 위해 절을 짓고 부처의 법을 설하며
중생을 공경하고, 곤경에서 구제하면
불국토를 장엄하는 보살과 보살을 장엄하는 중생이 생겨

신라가 고구려 침략을 막기 위해 봉림사를 지으며
보살의 위력으로 신라를 구제하면
역시 보살과 중생이 나뉘는 상이 생겨

내가 이렇게 했다는 상에 머물지 않으며
소리, 향기, 맛, 접촉, 법 등에 머무는 마음이 끊기면
마음을 잘 작동시키는 바른 이치 생겨

웨이드(Wade)는 호국사찰 봉림사에 머물며
봉황새를 꿈꾼다면
색, 성향, 미, 촉, 법 등의 상이 생겨

한양에서 웨이드가 독경에서 한 번 이기며
'내가 이렇다'라는 상에 머물지 않았다면
색, 성향, 미, 촉, 법을 다스리는 이치 생겨

Where Buddha Edified Is Solemn, But Not Solemn

By building a temple teaches the speech of Buddha to aide mankind
Respect mankind and aide mankind in difficulties
Mankind letting Bosals solemn and Bosals let Buddhist world magnificent appear

The Silla built the Bongrimsa to defend the Koguryeo attacking their land
When Bosals' power save the Silla areas
There would raise an idea to differentiate Bosals and mankind as divider

No staying at the idea what I did this deed
When the mind staying at sound, scent, taste, contact, and rules stops
The right reasons operating mind appear

Wade stayed at the Bongrimsa temple that patriotic spirit breathed
When he dreams to be one of phoenix birds
The images staying at sound, scent, taste, contact, and rules appear

In the capital city Wade once won in a contest of sutra recited
If he did not stay at the idea 'what I did this'
The right reasons controlling sound, scent, taste, contact, and rules appear

황하강의 모래 수

황하강의 모래 수만큼의 강에는 모래 수가 얼마나 될까
그만큼 많은 강들의 모래 수는 표현이 불가하고
그 모래 수만큼의 삼천 대천세계 보물을 보시하면 무량 복덕을 얻게 될까

세존 경전을 배워서 남에게 설명하면 복덕이 크지 않을까
경전을 타인에게 가르치고 널리 전하면 그 복덕이 크다고
그 복덕은 삼천 대천세계 보물의 보시보다 배가 될까

표현력이 풍부하고 열정적인 게일은 얼마나 많이 도전해 보았을까
말없이 열심히 노력하고
그렇게 많은 사람들을 위해 노래하면 무량 복덕을 얻을까

게일은 황하강의 모래 수꽃 수만큼 많은 경연대회를 왜 무심하게 보낼까
활동적이면서도 과묵하고
인정 많고 충실하니 공덕천*을 기다렸을까

게일의 노랫소리는 영주산 정상에 닿을까
목청은 청아키도 쇠를 긁는 것 같기도 하고
중생들이 그 레퍼토리를 언제 선호하게 될까

* 공덕천: 복덕을 주는 여신. 아름다운 얼굴에 럭셔리한 보관을 쓰고 여의주를 들고 있음

The Number of Sands of the Whangha River

How many are the sands if the number of river were the same as sands' of the Whangha river
The numbers of the sands are speechless based on the river numbers
Can donating treasures as much as the sands get the reward of virtues

You will get the reward of virtue by learning Buddha sutras for others or
If you teach and spread the sutras for others
The reward of virtue would be double amounts

Is Gale who expresses fluently and energetically
Gale is trying hard without talking complains
Does he wait for the Goddess of Good Luck for his mercies

Why he let go of the contest opportunities as many as spring flower
Although he is active and show reticence stands
He might wait for the reward of virtue and wisdom from the goddess

Did Gale's singing voice reach to the top of the Mt. Youngjusan tower
His voice is beautiful clearly and scratching iron sometimes
When does mankind get to prefer his repertories

법문이 일어나는 그곳

깨친 진리 담긴 게송을 설할지라도 그곳은 부처님 모신 곳
누가 사구게를 수지 독송하면 최상의 법을 성취하였으니
이 게송의 경전이 있는 곳이 부처님과 존중할 만한 제자들이 계신 곳

법문이 일어나는 그곳은 존중 정교가 중생을 만나는 곳
진리 담긴 게송들은 다이아몬드처럼 단단하고 섬광 가지니
게송을 설하는 곳은 공양을 올리는 법당과 같은 곳

범어사는 화엄경에 담긴 진리를 경전 / 게송으로 설하는 곳
포구와 해변을 가진 부산은 대다수 중생이 게송을 들으니
한국의 어느 도시보다 불교가 성한 곳

여기 동백꽃이 제일 먼저 계절을 알리는 곳
범어사에도 봄이 오니
법당마다 염불이 울려 퍼지는 곳

열정적이고 독립적인 대니가 게송 외우는 곳
뒤뜰에서 숯불 피우며 게송에 리듬을 넣으니
연기 따라 꽃향기 사찰 정원을 노니는 곳

Where the Buddha Teaching Is Told

Wherever phrases of enlightening truth is taught is the Buddha place
Who learned any four phrases of the truth achieved a best principle
Where the phrases and the sutra exist is Buddha and his students' place

Where the Buddha teaching is told is one meets a respected religion place
The phrases of Buddha teaching are hard like diamond and flash principle
Wherever the songs of the phrases are sung is like a temple hall place

Beomeosa in Busan teaches Whaum sutra and famous phrases to audience
Mankind listen to the phrases in Busan having beaches and harbor-side
The Buddhism is more popular in this city than other province

Camellia flowers tell spring season firstly in the province
Spring comes also to the Beomeosa temple
Every temple hall chants Buddhist prayers is resonating in the place

Energetic and independent Danny chants the prayers in this place
He put rhythms in the phrases while making fires with charcoal
Following the smoke spring flower scent is full of the place

지혜의 빛

여래께서 규범을 말씀하신 바가 없으며
다이아몬드처럼 깨지기 힘든 경전도 이름에 불과하며
지혜의 빛으로 참다운 지혜를 얻어 든 열반의 묘경도 이름에 불과하리라

여래께서 말씀하신 아주 작은 티끌은 그 이름에 불과하며
여래께서 말씀하신 세계 역시 그 이름에 불과하며
그러나 강 모래 수만큼의 목숨으로 보시해도 경전 가르치는 복이 더 크다 하시
니라

부처 가르침의 기본은 그 말씀 자체에도 상을 갖지 말며
지혜는 몸과 목숨보다 더 중요하며
부처님 말씀을 지혜로써 중생 구도하면 복덕이 더 크리라

부처 말씀 전하는 비로암은 비로라는 명칭에 상을 갖지 않으며
2500년을 초월해도 변치 않는 진리를 부처 말씀 속에서 찾으라 함이며
또 수천 번의 봄이 지나도 영원하리라

지혜의 빛에도 눈이 녹으며
이상주의적이고 품위 있는 스탠은
봄꽃에 대해 시를 쓰며
영광의 복덕이 올 날을 기다리리리라

Wisdom Lights

Buddha did not talked about norms in deed
The sutra name like diamond saying unbreakable is just a name
A nirvana reached by gaining real wisdom with wise lights is just a name

What Buddha says a 'tiny dust' is also just a name
What Buddha says 'world' in his teaching is also just a name as a word
But donating with countless lives is less valuable than teaching Buddhism

Do not take an image toward Buddha's teaching as the prime
Ones body or life is less valuable than wisdom as Buddha said
It is more rewards of virtue to aide mankind by Buddhism with wisdom

The Biroam spreading Buddhism does not have an image for the name
To find the abiding truth in the Buddha teaching over 2500 years passed
It is forever over another upcoming thousands of years of time

The snow was also melt in the Biroam
Idealistic and wise Stan writes poems on spring flowers blossomed
He is waiting for the day with the reward of virtue will come

모든 상에 대한 고정관념을 떠나면

부처님은 지극한 평화주의자이시다
나, 인간, 중생, 목숨의 실체가 있다는 고정관념을 떠나면
화가 나는 원한이 없어지니 고요하고 평화롭다

가르침의 어휘 조차에도 고정관념을 버리라고 하신다
이러한 가르침을 한 자도 빼지 않은 금강경을 수지한다면
지혜 바라밀로써 무량 무변 복덕을 예언하신다

마음에 머묾 없이 중생을 위해 보시하라신다
이 모든 상에 대한 고정관념을 떠나면
김영한은 이와 같이 보시하니 길상사는 영원하다

길상사에 계절 편지처럼 봄이 온다
중생의 실체라는 고정관념의 진(Jean)이가 떨면
봄바람이 살랑거리며 그 상을 버리라 한다

진이는 아직도 대중 앞에 서는 것이
떨린다
새싹 돋는 봄 가고 배롱나무꽃 피는
여름 오면
진이는 자신감 없는 '나'라는 상을
내려놓기 위해 기도한다

If One Leaves Where Every Stereotype Aappears

Buddha is a genuine pacifist
If stereotype that me (or human / mankind / life) has a true nature disappears
Angry grudge is disappeared, which brings calm and peace

Stereotypes on the words in his teaching should be gotten rid of at first
If one learned the Geumkanggyoung sutra that each point appears
He predicts limitless rewards of virtue through wisdom practice

He asks to donate for mankind without staying at 'me' done a best
If one leaves where every stereotype appears
Kim, Younghan donated like this, so the Gilsangsa be forever in peace

There comes spring in the Gilsangsa temple as a spring post
If Jean who did not throw the stereotype on mankind shivers
Spring wind asks him to throw the stereotype at once

Jean still shivers in front of audience most
If blossoming spring goes and summer comes with crape myrtle flowers
Jean prays to put down the image of 'me' without confidence

큰일

'나'라는 견해나 사람이라는 견해에 집착하고
중생이라는 생각이나 목숨이라는 생각에 집착하여도
큰일을 할 수 없고, 작은 일을 한다 해도 공덕이 없다

오전에 항하강 모래 수만큼 목숨을 보시하고
오후와 저녁에 또 항하강 모래 수만큼 목숨을 보시하여도
깨지지 않는 금강경을 이해하고 따르는 공덕이 두 배로 더 크다

이 경은 인류를 위해 일하는 사람을 위해 부처님이 설하고
이 말씀을 믿고 따르기만 하여도
자연히 그 공덕이 가치롭다

빌은 오전에 엄청난 구슬땀을 흘리고
오후와 저녁에도 또 엄청난 구슬땀을 흘려도
작은 일을 위해 노력하기에 공덕이 없다

빌은 왕산사에서 금강경을 외우고
'나'라는 생각을 내려놓고 올리는
기도
봄 지나, 여름 지나 그 공덕이
피어나리다

Great Works

If obsessing to 'me' idea or 'human' opinion
Either obsessing to mankind or living
Can achieve no great work, nor rewards of virtue and wisdom for tiny work

If donating lives as numbers of sands in Hangha river in the morn
And both donating that much lives in the afternoon and evening
Studying and practicing unbreakable Geumkanggyeong gets double luck

The Sutra is for the people to work for the world as Buddha's sermon
Only even believing in the Sermon and following
The reward of virtue and wisdom is naturally valuable luck

Bill sweats a lot for working in the morn
Also works very hard in the afternoon and evening
He worked for a little thing, so no reward of virtue and wisdom back

If Bill recites the Sutra in the Wangsansa and keeps going on
'Me' thinking puts down and keeps praying
Spring and summer goes by then bring the reward of virtue and wise luck

전생의 업장

전생의 업장이 두꺼워 남이 무시하고 멸시하더라도
깨지지 않는 금강경을 수지독송한다면
전생의 업장이 소멸되고 깨끗해진다고

팔만사천억 나유타*로 각 부처님께 공양하더라도
누군가가 깨지지 않는 금강경을 수지독송한다면
그 공양의 공덕보다 천만 억 배 이상을 넘는다고

남에게 보시하는 것이 바람직하다 하더라도
마음의 지혜(반야바라밀)를 수련하지 않는다면
자신을 그럴듯하게 포장하는 '아상'에 불과하다고

동화사의 책은 법당마다 공양 올리더라도
마음의 지혜를 수련하지 않는다면
이 봄에도 공덕을 받지 못할 것이라고

뚜렷한 목적의식이 있고 철저하더라도
잘 되게 해 달라고 기도만 한다면
다음 계절에도 공덕을 받지 못할
　것이라고

---

* 나유타: 10의 60승

Thick Karma

Although being neglected or despised from others due to thick karma
If you read the unbreakable Geumgang Sutra and carry it always
The karma gained before your birth will be disappeared and clean

Although paying much tribute to each 84 billion nayuta* Buddha
If someone reads the unbreakable Geumgang Sutra and carries it always
The rewards of virtue exceed the tribute's one as much as million billion

Although it is desirable to give mercy to others and Buddha
If you do not practice to get wisdom of mind every days
It is just making a decent 'me' image rather than

Although Jack pays tribute to each temple hall in the Dongwhasa
If he does not practice to get wisdom of mind every days
He does not get the reward of virtue and wisdom in this spring and so on

Although Jack has sense of target and thorough on his agenda
If he prays only for good luck and mercies
He may not obtain the reward of virtue and wisdom in following season

'나는 없다'에 통달하는 보살

가장 높고 바른 깨달음을 얻으려면
일체중생을 멸도했으나 실로 한 명도 구제하지 않았다고
내가 했노라 하면 보살이 아니라네

가장 높고 바른 깨달음으로 가는 실제 법이 있었다면
부처는 후세에 불릴 석가모니라는 이름을 얻지 못했다고
여래가 설한 일체법도 실제도 아니고 없는 것도 아니라네

부처가 설한 일체법이 다 불교 법이라면
일체법이 아닌 이유로 그 이름이 일체법이라고
'나는 없다'에 통달하는 보살이 진정한 보살이라 하네

이안이 나는 왜 어사화를 못 받냐고 원망하면
나, 사람, 중생, 목숨 등에 대한 집착이 있고
가장 높고 바른 깨달음을 얻을 수 없다네

이안이 최상의 경지에 이르려면
'나는 없다'라고, 모든 것은 실체가
　없다고
'마침내 나는 없다'를 통달하라 하시네

Bosal Who Masters 'I Do Not Exist'

To obtain the highest and righteous enlightenment
Have to be aware of nobody saved although all mankind were saved
You cannot become a Bosal if insisting 'I did good'

If there had been a real method for Buddha to get the enlightenment
He could not have named Seokgamoni the next generations have called
Buddha said that all sutra that Buddha spoke are not real nor non-existed

If all sutras that Buddha spoke were all of Buddhist
The name is 'all sutras' because it is not real but it just named
Who masters 'I do not exist' is a real Bosal Buddha said

If Ian resented why he could not obtain the victory flower hat
There are ideas of me, people, mankind, and life which he obsessed
So the highest and righteous enlightenment cannot be obtained

If Ian wants to reach to the highest and righteous moment
He must acknowledge there is no 'I' nor really exist everything existed
'There is no 'I' finally' must be mastered

마음은 시냇물 따라

옛님의 마음은 어디에 있는지 모른다
옛님에 대한 내 마음도 없어지고
과거의 마음은 얻을 수 없다

하루에도 많은 생각들이 일었다가 썰물처럼 빠져나간다
나간 마음은 이미 현재가 아니고
현재의 마음도 얻을 수 없다

어떤 인연이 문 앞에 올지도 모른다
그 인연에 대한 마음은 허상에 지나지 않고
미래의 마음도 얻을 수 없다

히스는 파계(把溪)사 골짜기 시냇물을 잡으려 한다
몇초 전의 시냇물은 이미 가버렸고
지금 다가온 시냇물은 손가락 사이로 빠져나간다

봄시냇물은 졸졸거리며 바삐
　어디론가 간다
아무것에도 집착하지 말라고
미래에도 그러할 것이라고 노래한다

* 파계(把溪): 시냇물을 잡다

Mind Following Water of Brook

Don't know where the ex-lover's mind is
My mind for the past was also disappeared
So the past mind cannot be gained

Tremendous thoughts have yielded and gone like ebb tides
Thinking gone was not already present mind
So the present mind cannot be gained

Don't know what kind of destinies visit your door steps
To imagine future destinies is just illusions dreamed
So the future mind cannot be gained

Heath tries to grasp water of brook running the Pagyesa valleys
The water of brook coming a few seconds before was already disappeared
The water of brook coming now is going through fingers and eluded

Spring water of brook is busily purling to somewhere down
Do not obsess to anything
Sings it will be so in the future among mankind

복덕 아닌 복덕

누구 보채, 누구 보채 기도 소리에
부처님께 복덕 달라고 보채는 것 같기도 하고
스님의 목소리는 카랑카랑하시네

삼천 대천세계의 칠보를 보시하는 것에
이 인연으로 복덕을 얻겠냐고 부처께서 질문하시고
그런 이유로는 복덕이 실재하지 않는다고 하시네

그러한 복덕이 없기에
부처께서는 복덕이 많다 하시고
복덕 아닌 복덕이라고 교화하시네

웨이드는 ego를 내려놓지 못하기에
봉림사 극락전에 행운을 달라고 기도하고
기도에 대한 복덕이 있는 것도 아니고 없는 것도 아님을 모르네

복덕 아닌 복덕의 부처님 말씀은 즉비*의
논리이기에
기도하면 복을 받을 수 있다고
거기에 매이지 말라고 하시네

---

* 즉비 논리: 금강경에서 부처님이 설한 법을 부처님이 설한 바가 아니라고 하면서 그 이름이라는 논리. 예: 복덕 아닌 복덕. 구족색신 즉비구족색신 시명 구족색신.

The Good Luck Which Was Not Real But Existed

Praying voice such as for John doe, and for somebody
It sounds like fretful praying as being reverse
The praying voice of the monk is clear and high-pitched

Tremendous treasures of three oceans were donated to a temple or else
Buddha asked whether there be a reward of virtue as the cause-effect ring
Buddha said there was not any reward of virtue for the reason existed

For the reason there was no good luck in Buddhist rhapsody
While Buddha said the person got a reward of virtue for the donating case
Buddha edified the good luck which was not real but existed

Because Wade could not put down his ego already
He prays for the reward of virtue at the Bongrimsa Paradise Hall or else
While not knowing rewards of virtue could exist or not for the prayed

Buddha's edification is based on the negation logic to go steady
In someway your praying might bring a reward of virtue or nothing else
So Buddha asked us not to get entangled

신체적 특성에 집착하지 말라

부처께서는 모든 형상이 제대로 갖춰져 있지만
눈에 보이는 것에 집착하지 말라고
얼굴 특성이나 신체 모습은 초월하라고

세계 어느 나라에서도 부처가 출현할 수 있지만
그 나라마다 생김 특징이 다 다르다고
그러니 신체적 특성도 형상도 떠나라고

같은 지역 같은 종족이라 하지만
각자의 생김과 각자의 개성은 다 다르다고
신체적 특성이나 얼굴 모습에 집착하지 말라고

데일은 목청 높여 열심히 기도하지만
목소리는 동굴같이 낮게 울려 탄식하고
스님의 청아한 목소리에만 집착하고

도선사를 에워싼 산야에는 봄이 왔지만
데일의 목소리는 누가 알아주냐고
데일의 개성에는 언제 봄이 오냐고

Do Not Obsess with Physical Characteristics

Although Buddha was furnished with all physical images
Do not be obsessed with what you see
Be free from face characteristics and physical figure

Although Buddha appears in any country with different images
Each ethnic characteristic differs as you see
Leave your stereotypes on physical images and figure

Although people with same ethnicity live in the same areas
Each owns different looks and personality
Do not obses with physical characteristics and face figure

Although Dale prays in high-pitched voices
He sighs because his voice lowers like cave echo as you may agree
He obsesses to clear and high-pitched voice of monks here

Although spring has come to hills surrounding the Doseonsa temple halls
Who recognizes Dale's voice as a guarantee
When does spring come to Dale's characteristic here

설법 아닌 설법의 여름

부처께서는 말씀하셨지만 말씀한 것이 없다 하시네
설법 아닌 설법이라네
말씀하신 법 이름이 설법이라 하시네

부처님의 주옥같은 설법도 다 깨뜨리시네
설법에 집착하지 말라 하시네
아집을 버리라고 솔선수범하시네

누가 부처님을 믿겠는가 묻는다면 정녕 불교를 모르는 것이라네
그들은 본디 중생 아닌 중생이라네
그 이름이 중생이라네

어머니는 계속 울면 반성이 아니라 하시네
반성 아닌 반성이라 하시네
반성은 말로만 하는 것이 아니라네

게일은 어머니 몰래 레퍼토리를
  쌓고 있네
게일은 늘 어머니께 반성 아닌
  반성을 하네
아집을 버리려고 노력하지만 아직은
  멀었네

Summer of the Buddhist Sermon That Is Not Sermon

Buddha says there is no sermon although Buddha had spoken
So to speak. Buddha sermons that are not sermons
The name of Buddha's speech is Buddha sermon

Buddha insists all gems of his sermon must be broken
Do not obsess to his sermons
He takes an initiative and sets an example to get rid of being stubborn

You do not know Buddhism if asking who would believe in the spoken
The 'who' is mankind that is not mankind as it begins
The name is mankind until they enlighten

Mother says it is not regrets on wrongdoing if you keep crying then
She says the regret is not the regret on your wrongdoing owns
Regretting is not only talking but doing right later on

Gael adds up gems of repertory while his mom does not listen
Gael repeats regretting to her, were not real ones
Here is long to go while trying to get rid of being stubborn

얻을 것이 없는 법의 여름

제일 큰 법을 이루고서도 그 이름이 큰 법일 뿐
부처께서는 모든 가능성을 열어두고
이루심을 즉비로 깨 버리시네

부처님의 중요한 명제는 그 이름이 명제일 뿐
깨달음에 대한 집착마저도 내려놓고
깨달음의 이름이 깨달음이라 하시네

깨달음에서 조그마한 법조차도 얻을 만한 것이 없을 뿐
가장 높고 바른 깨달음이라고
돌리고 돌리시네

대니는 깨닫고서 조금 깨달음 맛을 본 것뿐
깨달음에 대한 집착마저도 내려놓지 못하고
깨버림의 벅차오름을 모르네

여름은 한 철일 뿐
다음 계절은 눈앞으로 오고
깨버림의 벅차오름은 아직 여기에 없네

Summer of the Buddhist Sermon That Cannot Be Obtain

Although achieving an eventual goal, Buddha says its name is the one
He opens all possibilities over hundreds thousands decades
He uses his denial logic to discard his achievement

His important proposition is called just proposition as the one
He put down even the obsession for enlightenment as a way to the roads
He calls enlightenment as the name of enlightenment

There is no tiny logic to gain enlightening one
The highest and right enlightening deeds
Buddha twisted and twisted his words to get a real enlightenment

Although Danny got enlightened, he tasted only a little one
He could not put down his obsession to the roads
He does not know an overflowing joy gained by breaking the illusion moment

Summer is only season one
Next season is coming in hands
An overflowing joy by breaking the illusion is not yet in this moment

깨달음에 이르는 법은 평등하여

깨달음에 이르는 법은 평등하여 높고 낮음이 없고
그 이름이 가장 높고 바른 깨달음일 뿐
모든 존재가 가지고 있는 이치는 평등하다고

일체 선법을 닦는 자세는 너다, 나다가 없고
자아의식, 차별의식, 열등의식, 한계의식 등도 없을 뿐
이 모든 의식이 사라진 마음 자세로 닦아야 한다고

남자, 여자, 선행, 종교, 음식 등 일체가 즉비라고
부처께서는 선한 일 수행에 집착하면 선한 일이 아닐 뿐
그 이름이 선한 일이라고

깨끗한 마음으로 선행하여 마음을 닦으라고
스탠은 '나'라는 실체에 집착할 뿐
찰나 찰나의 사건에 '나'라는 실체를 붙들고

높고 낮음이 없는 평등한 선법을 모르고
스탠은 가장 높고 바른 깨달음을 수행할 뿐
찰나적 사건 관계에 집착하니 갈 길이 멀고

The Way to Gain an Enlightening is Equal

The way to gain an enlightening is equal, so no high nor low
The name is only the highest and right enlightenment
The reason of every being's possession is equal

There is no 'I' nor 'you' in the practicing attitude of all Buddhist law
There were no self-awareness, no discrimination, nor limit settlement
Practice only with the attitude to discard these consciousness all

All unites such as man, woman, or good deed are under 'denial-logic' law
The good deed is no longer good when you obsess to the element
The name is only good deed what Buddhas call

Practice your mind by doing goods with clean heart from the low
Stan obsesses only to the substance of 'I' statement
Holding the substance of 'I' moment by moment toward incidental real

He does not know the equal good practice without high and low
Stan practices only the highest and right enlightenment
Obsesses to the relations of the moment, so he is far from the goal

큰 복과 비교 불가한 지혜

수미산*만큼 보시하는 사람의 복덕은 얼마나 클까
금강경 사구게**만을 읽고 외워 타인에게 설하면 그 복덕은 얼마나 될까
전자의 복덕은 후자의 것의 백의 하나에도 미치지 못한다네

부처님은 왜 복을 지혜와 비교할 수 없다고 하셨을까
경전 수지의 복덕이 최고라고 하셨을까
부처님 지혜로 살아가는 복덕이 최고라 하시네

전 재산을 부처님 말씀 전하는 길상사 건립에 바친 김영한의 복은 얼마나 될까
길상사에서 부처님 경전을 전할 수 있었으니 그 복덕은 얼마나 클까
김영한의 복덕은 어마어마하겠네

대중을 위로하기 위해 부르는 노래의 복덕은 얼마나 클까
대중의 고통을 없애주기 위해 전하는 사구게만큼 클까
부처님 지혜로 살아가는 복덕이 최고라네

대중에게 바칠 노래를 연마하는 진이의 복덕은 얼마나 될까
노래 연습으로 쌓인 진이의 고통은 누가 풀어 줄까
길상사의 부처님 말씀은 진이를 기다리고 있네

---

* 수미산: 불교식 세계에서 제일 큰 산
** 사구게: 금강경의 핵심사상을 간략한 4구의 형식으로 나타낸 게송

Wisdom That Could be Incomparable to the biggest Lotto

How much is the luck for whom donated as much as the biggest Mt.
How much luck is for teaching the cores of the Diamond Sutra to others
The reward of the former cannot reach one hundredth of the latter

Why Buddha said the wisdom could be incomparable to lucks of Mt.
Why the luck of reading / understanding the Sutra is the best among others
Living with Buddha wisdom is the best good luck as the matter

How much luck is for Kim, Younghan donated whole fortunes to build a temple at last
How much luck is for delivering the Sutra through the Temple to others
The reward of virtue for Kim, Younghan must be enormous bigger

How much reward is for singing to console others in a concert
Is it big luck to deliver the core Sutra to unburden agonies of others
To live with Buddha wisdom must be the best reward as the matter

How much reward is for Jean practicing singing for mankind in a concert
Who console Jean's agonies while practicing singing songs for others
The Buddha's words are waiting for Jean to help himself smoother

교화해도 교화한 바가 없다시네

좋은 일을 하여도 한 바 없이
물가에 데려간 말들이 스스로 물을 마셨다고
'내가 도왔다' 하지 않으시네

나, 인간, 중생, 목숨 등에 집착한 바 없이
'나'에 집착하는 범부도 있고
그러나 범부는 단지 이름이 범부라고 하시네

망상과 집착으로 인하여 스스로 속박하는바
고통을 받고 사는 것이 범부라고
고통의 원인을 던져버리면 범부를 탈피한다 하시네

빌은 자신 없는 자아에 집착하는바
사람 앞에 서는 것이 두렵고
중생들 앞에서 노래를 하려면 바들바들 떠네

노래한 바 없이 노래하면 되는바
자신 없는 자아를 내려놓고
고통의 원인을 던져버리고 노래만
즐기라 하시네

Buddha Who Denied His Teaching Mankind Although He Did

Although giving mercies, pretends doing nothing
The horses drank water themselves with taking them to the river
Do not say 'I helped them'

Do not obsess with me, you, people, and living
But there are ordinary persons obsessing with 'ego' owner
Buddha said their name is 'ordinary person' to call them

People enchain themselves with nursing delusion and obsessing
Ordinary persons are pain taker
Buddha says they will be free if they throw the cause of pain on them

Helpless ego is what Bill is obsessing
He is afraid of standing in front of audience
He is shivering when singing in front of them

He could sing while pretending he is not singing
Put down the helpless ego further
He could enjoy singing by throwing the cause of pain on him

신체적 특징으로 표현될 수 없는 부처

부처님 몸대로 조성된 형상불이 보이는가
그러나 법신은 형상이 아니다
고통은 형상에 집착하고 마음을 모르는 데서 온다

세존은 32가지 신체적 특징이 있다 하는가
32상을 가졌다고 해서 다 세존이 아니다
부처님 지혜와 복덕 여부에서 온다

형색으로, 음성으로 부처를 보는가
그것은 부처를 보는 방법이 아니다
그 길에서는 여래를 볼 수 없다

잭은 형상에 집착하는가
긴 머리와 큰 키를 가졌다고 해서 로커는 아니다
형색과 음성에서는 그것을 볼 수 없다

잭은 고음에 집착하는가
꽥꽥거린다고 로커는 아니다
로커로서의 자성이 없으면
그 이름을 얻을 수 없다

Buddha Cannot Be Characterized Physically

Can you see the statue of the Buddha built on the physical characteristics
But the Buddha body in the buddhist world is not a shape
Agony comes from obsessing to a shape and ignoring mind

Did the Buddha have 32 physical characteristics
We do not call Buddha somebody having the 32 kinds of shape
It depends on the Buddha wisdom and the reward of virtue as a key ground

Do you see the Buddha as body or voice characteristics
That is not the way to see the Buddha characteristics
We cannot see the Buddha in that road

Does Jack obsess to physical characteristics
Long hair and height are not the only rockers' characteristics
We cannot see it in body or voice standard

Is it high tone that Jack obsesses
Just yelling is not belong to rockers
Without original nature as rockers the name cannot be obtained

단절과 소멸의 초월

깨달음에는 끊음도 멸함도 없다
그러니 단절과 소멸을 초월하라
모든 현상이 여실하게 존재한다

부처님에게 32상은 있는 것도 아니며 없는 것도 아니다
부처님이 32상을 갖춰 깨달음을 이루었다고 말하지 말라
있는 것과 없는 것이 합하는 중도를 가르치신다

바른길에는 긍정도 부정도 치우침이 없다
또한 부처가 구족상 없이 가장 높은 깨달음을 얻은 것으로 하지 말라
진리의 깨달음에 대한 마음을 낸 사람은 단멸상을 설하지 않는다

이안의 마음에는 깨달음이 없다
어사화에 집착하지 말라
가고 옴에 자유로워 마음에 걸림이 없어야 한다

이안의 장래 목표에도 진리에 대한
깨달음이 없다
가장 높은 자리에 가기 위해 단멸을
초월하라
일체의 모든 형상을 형상이 아닌 줄
알면 그때 우승이 보인다

Transcend Cutting off and Extinction

There is no cutting off nor extinction in enlightenment
So transcend cutting off and extinction
Each phenomenon exists as itself

Speaking of Buddha, the 32 physical shapes does not exist nor no-existent
Do not talk Buddha with 32 shapes got to enlighten
He teaches the mid that combines being exist and no-existent thereof

There is no affirmation nor negation in the righteous way and sight
Do not take Buddha without the 32 shapes got the highest enlightenment
Who wants to be enlightened does not teach images of extinction and cutting off

There is no wish for Ian to gain an enlightenment
Please do not obsess to the victory hat with flowers on
There should no barrier in mind in comings and goings

There is no wish nor goal for Ian to gain a true enlightenment
To get the top rank needs to transcend cutting off and extinction
You will see a victory by taking all phenomena are not thereof

받지도 탐하지도 않는 복덕

보살이 항하의 모래 수만큼 세계에 칠보를 보시하고
어떤 이가 모든 법이 무아임을 알고 인욕을 성취하면
이 보살의 공덕은 앞의 보살보다 더 뛰어나다고

복덕을 받을 것으로 기대하지도 않고
탐하는 마음도 없다면
진정한 보살이라고

모든 보살들은 복덕을 누리지 않고
지은 복덕에 탐욕을 내거나 집착하지 않는다면
부처는 보살이 복덕을 누리지 않는다고

Heath는 뛰어난 재능으로 보시하고
재능기부에 대한 복덕을 기대한다면
진정한 복덕을 받을 수 없다고

Heath가 엄청난 재물로 보시를 하고
그 이름을 영원히 남기고자 한다면
인욕으로 일체법이 무아임을 아는
이보다 그 복덕이 적다고

The Reward of Virtue That is Neither Received nor Coveted

One donates treasures like the number of sand in a river to the world
The other succeeds tolerating greed while living without ego
The latter's rewards of virtue exceeds the former

No expect to receive the virtue reward
And if there is no greedy ego
S/he is a true saint of the Buddha follower

All Buddha follower do not enjoy the reward of virtue indeed
Without greed on the reward of virtue nor obsession
So Buddha says his followers do not enjoy the reward of virtue appear

Heath serves his talent to the world
But if he expects the reward of virtue too
He cannot receive a real reward of virtue from the behavior

Heath donates a huge mount of wealth to the world
If he desires to leave his name behind too
His reward is less than tolerating greed and living no ego doer

부처의 진리는 가고 옴이 없다

어떤 사람이 여래(진리)는 오기도 하고 가기도 한다고 하면
그 사람은 부처가 설한 뜻을 이해하지 못한 것인바
부처의 다른 이름, 여래는 오고 감이 없다고

그 사람이 여래는 오기도 하고 가기도 한다고 하면
여래란 어디로부터 오는 것도 없고 가는 것도 없는바
마음대로 가고 오고 자유자재하다고

부처가 진리로서 행동 형태는 왕래가 아니라면
와도 온 것이 없고 가도 간 것이 없는바
그 이름 여래는 본래 그 모습 그대로의 자리가 오는 것이라고

Wade가 여래에 대해 미래에 올 것이라고 한다면
여래의 진리에 어두운바
진리 구현의 기회를 놓치게 될 것이라고

Wade는 여래가 강 저 너머에서
올 것이라고 믿는다면
Wade 역시 물을 건널 것인바
와도 온 흔적이 없는 기회를 놓치게
될 것이라고

Buddha Truth's Acting Forms

If somebody says Buddha truth is to come and go
S/he misunderstands the Buddha speeches
His other name, the coming nature itself or truth does not mean 'come or move'

If S/he insists the coming nature itself or truth does come and go
The coming nature itself or truth does not come from somewhere nor goes
The truth comes and goes as it likes, which does freely move

If the forms of Buddha as the truth are not the come-and-go
Although it comes there is no what it comes, the same happens to 'goes'
The name 'Yeorae' means that the figure of nature comes to the place as it is

If Wade says Yeorae will come in future too
He is in black night for truths
Which will let go the opportunity to make the truth active

If Wade believes Yeorae will come over a river far go
Wade also will cross the river as he believes
The opportunity that comes without the trace will go like a wave

진리와 형상은 하나이다

작은 먼지들이 실제로 숫자로 말할 수 있는 것이라면
여래는 먼지라고 말하지 않는다고
먼지 수가 곧 먼지의 숫자가 아니라고. 그 이름이 먼지 수라 하시네

세계가 실제로 있는 것이라면
한 덩어리의 모양이겠지만 끊임없이 변한다고
삼천대천세계는 세계가 아니라 그 이름이 세계라 하시네

가장 작은 먼지서부터 끊임없이 변화하는 지구에 대한 실상을 파악한다면
오로지 마음속에 잘못 인식되어있는 상념들이 있다고
면면히 흐르는 하나로 통합된 이치를 찾으라고 하시네

Dale의 마음속에 온갖 번뇌망상들이 있다면
생각하다 보면 마음에 하나의 구체적인 현상으로 굳어진다고
고정된 실체 없음의 참모습을 보라 하시네

각 형상마다 진리가 똑같이 들어있다면
작은 먼지에 대한 상도 지우라고
가장 큰 지구라는 상도 지우라고 하시네

The Truth is One Whatever Each Shape Has Its Form

If fine dust can be counted as real number
Yeorae (another name of Buddha) does not call it fine dust
The fine dust number is not the number, but the name is the one

If the world is really existing one as the bigger
It could be a lump shape, which is changing in constant
The oceans-rivers-continents is not a world, but the name is the one

If we find each real state from 'dust as a tiniest' to 'the earth as the bigger'
There are only wrong recognized notions in our thought
Yeorae asks to find the unified truth unceasing under each one

If Dale has various agony in his mind and falls into delusion of grandeur
His thinking on it, which hardens as a concrete phenomenon in his heart
Yeorae asks to see the real form without fixed nature of each one

If each form has the same truth as equalizer
Yeorae asks us to erase the form on dust as a smallest
Asks us to erase the form on earth as a biggest one

고정된 것은 진리에 있어서마저도 없다

자아, 상대, 중생, 목숨 등이 있다는 견해를 여래가 설했다고 한다면
그것은 여래가 말한 뜻을 알지 못한 것
예를 들어 그 이름을 말씀한 것일 뿐

가장 높은 깨달음을 얻고자 한다면
일체법에 대해 꼭 이와 같이 알고, 보며, 믿고 이해할 것
법이라는 관념(법상)마저도 내지 말아야 할 뿐

법이라는 관념은 법이라는 관념이 아니라고 설하셨다면
그 이름이 법이라는 관념이라는 것
부처가 설한 법에 대한 고정된 관념도 쓸어내야 할 뿐

Gale이 자아를 지키고 상대를 본다면
그것은 승리의 원리를 깨닫지 못한 것
과정과 결과에 번뇌 망상만 키울 뿐

Gale이 가장 높은 정상에 오르고자 하면
매 순간 진리의 속성에 대해 파악하고
  믿어야 할 것
일체법에 대한 고정된 관념도 쓸어내야
  할 뿐

There is No Fixed One in the Truth at All

If Yeorae (another name of Buddha) explained about ego, others, mankind, and life
Which is not understanding what Yeorae meant
He used only each name as an example

If the highest enlightenment is to be obtained to be safe
You need to know, see, trust, and understand all Yeorae logic-fact
Not to make any notion on each Yeorae's example

If being explained the notion of truth is not the notion of truth
The notion of truth is only the name
The stereotype on what Yeorae explained all the truths be swept away

If Gale keeps ego and see his rivals with being unsafe
Which is the sign that he did not recognized the principle of tournament
Only will raise agonies and delusions to become large

If Gale would get to the highest hill in his life
Must grisp and trust the attributes of truth every moment
Any stereotype on all the truths must be swept away from his judge

교화를 위해 여러 모습으로 나타나는 응화신은 진리가 아니다

한량없는 칠보를 가득 보시하더라도
보살심으로 이경의 사구게만이라도 다른 사람에게 몸소 보여준다면
보살심 수행의 복이 칠보 보시 복을 능가할지라

어떻게 남을 위해 설명해 주더라도
상을 취하지 말고 생색내지 않고 행동으로써 보여준다면
관념에 집착하지 말고 흔들림 없이 할지라

일체 조작적 정의가 있는 법은 꿈, 환영, 물거품, 그림자와 같기도
이슬과 같고 저 번갯불과 같다고 본다면
응당 이같이 관찰하고 유위법 그 너머를 볼 줄 알지라

Danny는 눈에 일차적으로 비쳐진 현상에 집착하기도
세상을 보는데 일차원적인 관점으로만 본다면
그 너머에 있는 것을 놓치게 될지라

Danny가 응화신의 꿈을 꾸고 환영을 보고
믿기도
그것이 깨달음의 유일한 유위법이라면
달이 숨으면 응화신은 사라지니 어떻게
흔들림 없이 살지라

The Various Appearance of Expedient Figures to Educate Is not the Real Buddha

Although limitless treasures are donated
The key points of the Sutra are explained to others with Bodhisattva mind
The latter reward of virtue is outstanding than the former

How to explain the key points of the Diamond Sutra to others mind
To take no fixed-images in practicing without doing yourself proud
Practice steady without obsessing to any stereotype on the Buddha spoke earlier

It is like a dream, bubble, or shadow that a truth operationally established
It would be dewdrop or a flash of lightning to be seemed
Must see like this way and consider beyond truths Buddha spoke earlier

Danny might obsesses to a phenomenon primarily lighted to his eyes
If one-dimensional sight were used to see the world
He might let go of the key beyond the truth mentioned much simpler

Danny might have a delusive dream and believe the Buddha image represented
If it were only the enlightening way he operated
The Buddha image disappears in hidden Moon, how to live steadier

ABOUT THE AUTHOR

Kim, Youn-Ock (김윤옥)

BA & MA, Busan National University, Korea
MA & Ed.D. University of West Virginia, USA
Teaching in Gongju National Univ. of Ed.
Professor Emeritus, Gongju National Univ. of Ed.

부산대학교 학사, 석사
미국 웨스트버지니아주립대학교 석사, 박사
공주교육대학교 교수 역임
현재 공주교육대학교 명예교수

마음의 꽃수들 Flower Fancy Works of Mind

2023년 1월 25일 1판 1쇄 인쇄
2023년 1월 30일 1판 1쇄 발행

저　자 : 김윤옥
발행인 : 한정주
발행처 : 교육과학사

경기도 파주시 광인사길 71
전화 : (031) 955-6956~8 / 팩스 : (031) 955-6037
Home-page : www.kyoyookbook.co.kr
E-mail : kyoyookbook@daum.net / kyoyook@chol.com
등록 : 1970년 5월 18일 제2-73호

ISBN 978-89-254-1747-9
Printed in Korea.
정가 18,000원